MAPPING THE FUTURE

READER'S GUIDE

by
Howard Zeiderman

Published by
TOUCHSTONES®
DISCUSSION PROJECT

Other Available Touchstones Program Materials

Elementary School
Touchpebbles Volume A (Student and Teacher editions)
Touchpebbles Volume B (Student and Teacher editions)

Middle School
Touchstones Volume A (Student and Teacher editions)
Touchstones Volume B (Student and Teacher editions)
Touchstones Volume C (Student and Teacher editions)
Courage to Care, Building Community through Service (our community service
    volume for middle grades) (Student and Teacher editions)
Where'd They Get That Idea?: Issues and Ideas in Science and Mathematics - Vol. I
    (Student and Teacher editions)

High School
Touchstones Volume I (Student and Teacher editions)
Touchstones Volume II (Student and Teacher editions)
Investigating Mathematics (Student edition)
Readings in Social Studies (Anthology)
SAT Preparation for Critical Reading (Student edition)

Post-secondary
Mapping the Future (Reader's guide and Leader's supplement)
New Landscapes (Student edition)
The Compass (College edition)

Other volumes
Courage to Care, Strength to Serve (our community service volume for
    older grades or adults) (Student and Leader editions)
The Compass (Executive level)
Discussion Leadership: Getting Started (Leader's guide)

In support of your work to bring dialogue, increased critical thinking, collaborative leadership, and community to your students, Touchstones Discussion Project offers educators a range of professional development services. Contact us for more information or to schedule an introductory presentation.

About the Touchstones® Discussion Project

The Touchstones Discussion Project is a nonprofit organization founded on the belief that all people can benefit from the listening, speaking, thinking, and interpersonal skills gained by engaging in active, focused discussions. Since 1984, Touchstones has helped millions of students and others develop and improve these skills in school, work, and life. For more information about the Touchstones Discussion Project, visit www.touchstones.org.

©2003, 2006, 2012
by Touchstones Discussion Project
PO Box 2329
Annapolis, Maryland 21404
800-456-6542
www.touchstones.org

ISBN: 978-1-937742-27-0

Acknowledgments

No work is created by one person. Countless people and circumstances influence the genesis of the idea and the production of the work. My work with the reading group that met for ten years at the New York Harvard Club and the group that still meets in Georgetown was the source of many of the issues and the catalyst for many of the thoughts contained in *Mapping the Future*. Also, the reading group in San Francisco that first piloted the material was an invaluable source of encouragement and a spur to the book's shape and completion. I also thank my colleagues at Touchstones for their willingness to brainstorm, their depth of experience with discussion groups, and their insistence that we never cut corners, either theoretical or practical, in producing a work that could open new possibilities for people. — *Howard Zeiderman*

Touchstones would like to thank the following for their help in the publication of this volume.

The National Gallery of Art, Washington, D.C., for permission to reproduce *Woman Holding a Balance* by Johannes Vermeer and *Diamond Painting in Red, Yellow, and Blue* by Piet Mondrian.

Harper and Row Publishers for permission to reprint the following:

Pages 62–68 from *Physics and Beyond* by Werner Karl Heisenberg. Translated by Arnold J. Pomerans. Copyright 1971 by Harper and Row.

Pages 14–17 from *The Question Concerning Technology and Other Essays* by Martin Heidegger. Translated by William Lovitt. Copyright 1977 by Harper and Row.

Alfred A. Knopf for permission to reprint pages 34–38 from *The Plague* by Albert Camus. Translated by Stuart Gilbert. Copyright 1948 by Stuart Gilbert.

About the Author

Howard Zeiderman is a co-founder and President of the Touchstones® Discussion Project. He is also senior faculty member at St. John's College in Annapolis, Maryland and for five years directed the Executive Seminar Program for the Aspen Institute. Zeiderman has 40 years of experience teaching in St. John's College's "great books" seminar program and extensive hands-on experience leading discussions with executives, managers, college students, graduate students, teachers, prison inmates, and seniors. He also conducts executive seminars for the Washington, D.C. Executive Discussion Group, the Aspen Institute, the Federal Executive Institute, and the New York Executive Discussion Group. Zeiderman has had extensive experience conducting workshops worldwide and is a leader in teaching educators and executives in how to create participant-centered discussion environments, run effective and inclusive seminars, and foster collaborative leadership.

In the past 30 years as a primary author of the Touchstones Discussion Project, Zeiderman has developed more than 14 volumes of texts and nine instructional guides to form the core of the Touchstones' curriculum. He has also conducted more than 400 workshops and served as a guest lecturer to many colleges and organizations. He received the Award of Merit from the Alumni Association of St. John's College in Annapolis in recognition of his creativity in and dedication to fostering education for all people through the Touchstones Discussion Project.

Contents

Stage 1: Authority and Expertise

Stage 2: Legitimate Speakers

Stage 3: Listening and Understanding

Stage 4: Leadership, Participation, and Commitment

Introduction

The Touchstones Discussion Project enables participants to become more self-aware, reflective, and responsible world citizens. Rapid advances in technology and the increased interdependence of nations and problems have placed current forms of organization—from national governments to local neighborhoods—under enormous strain. Both as individuals and as members of communities, we are faced with a choice: we can either let circumstances impose new structures upon us, or we can seize the initiative and help create new structures. To undertake the latter responsibly on either the personal or communal level, however, we need more than a new plan of action, strong leadership, or even the genuine desire to enact proactive change. Seizing the initiative for positive change requires in each individual self-knowledge and reflection on the deepest and most fundamental assumptions of our world. Before we can change, we must first know who we are. The Touchstones Discussion Project allows us to experience the transformation that occurs when individuals learn to learn together, explore their world together, and collectively map strategies and create the skills necessary to move ahead. You are about to undertake this journey. You will begin to map the future.

The assumptions we must examine critically—if we are to achieve self-awareness and sustain the possibilities of real changes in perspective—are those with which we are so familiar that we hardly notice, much less question, them. For example, we assume that experts are the primary source of knowledge and that their knowledge gives us the best resource to solve problems in the most efficient and effective way. We have been taught to defer to experts throughout our lives. However, without a reevaluation of such assumptions and other basic ways of thinking, even our innovative attempts to create profound change will fail to achieve their goals. Precisely because they are so pervasive yet so unquestioned, our most fundamental beliefs can limit our attempts to implement new ideas. We will travel the same worn-out paths of action unless we exert ourselves to view the entire terrain of our possibilities. A strategy is therefore necessary to bring our assumptions sufficiently into the open so that they can be examined. Certainly this examination need not lead us to the conclusion that all our most basic attitudes and ways of interacting with the world should be abandoned or radically altered. Some may even be our allies in our attempt to chart and navigate the unfamiliar terrain ahead. To make such judgments, however, we must learn to see what is so familiar that we often overlook it.

The Touchstones Method is just such a strategy. As a Touchstones participant, you will explore strategically selected texts within a specially designed format of discussion. This experience enables participants to do the following:

- Explore the unseen paradigms of their lives
- Learn to work with others across boundaries
- Explore and modify their conceptual frameworks
- Assess current perspectives, habits, and practices with a critical eye
- Take on and encourage cooperative forms of leadership and action
- Learn how to learn

You will achieve these goals as you move through the four stages to becoming a full participant in a Touchstones Discussion.

Moving through Stages

For success in Touchstones, all members of the group must eventually participate fully in the group discussions. Typically, full participation means that each member of the group feels free to express an opinion and does so. However, full participation in Touchstones is actually much more complex. It involves each member of the group leading the discussion as well as simply taking part. One of the goals of Touchstones is to give each participant an introduction to, and practice with, cooperative leadership through engaged participation in discussion. In such a situation, there is no single leader from whom all authority derives and with whom all responsibility ultimately rests. Rather, leadership in a discussion moves through the group as first one member and then another contributes the ideas and energy that give direction to an investigation. Participation in Touchstones will give individuals the opportunity to both experience and reflect on a shared form of leadership. This sharing ultimately emerges along with the ability of the group itself, with the active participation of all its members, to determine the shape of an inquiry. The units in this volume are divided into four sections, each of which represents a stage in reaching this goal.

Stage 1: Authority and Expertise

Throughout our lives, most of us have been encouraged and trained to listen to the teacher, the expert, or the authority. Following this encouragement is useful because we often need to gain the knowledge these people have mastered. However, an unfortunate consequence is that we come to feel that we cannot legitimately speak about topics we have not studied in an official capacity either as part of formal education or professional life. When we speak as nonspecialists, in the back of our intellectual consciences we sense that we are treading on someone else's territory. We are constantly ready to apologize for overstepping and to defer to experts. However, many of the deepest issues facing us—relationships with others, diversity, and living in a global society—are precisely ones for which there are no experts. To explore and deal with these issues, we will have to learn to cooperate with other nonexperts.

Thus our first task in Mapping the Future will be to overcome this attitude of reliance on expertise without just speaking irresponsibly. What can we speak responsibly about? What do we really know? The one topic on which we are all authorities is ourselves. However, personal storytelling alone will not advance the goals of this group. We need to find a middle ground between demonstrating the expertise associated with a branch of knowledge and simply sharing our personal stories. This middle ground comes from the interrelation between the text and our experiences. The texts in Stage 1 all concern authority, expertise, and the power associated with those qualities; the experience we bring to these texts is our struggle in dealing with the very issues they discuss within the context of the discussion group. Thus a complex interrelation between text and process emerges, and you will see this throughout Mapping the Future. Discussion of the texts in Stage 1 will assist us in depersonalizing our experience and thereby making it available to others. Furthermore, the particular experiences being depersonalized will be those involving our struggles with authority and expertise. This first stage covers the first five units.

Stage 2: Legitimate Speakers

The second stage begins with the recognition that we, although hardly experts on every topic, are nevertheless able to speak responsibly. A difficulty arises, however, because we all tend to segment the group into "legitimate" and "nonlegitimate" speakers. That is, we trust the words and efforts of some members of the group and believe that we can learn from them, whereas we treat with far less respect the words and efforts of others. This delineation is perfectly understandable. That is how we choose friends and colleagues. By the beginning of the second stage, each of us imagines that we and a few others have reached a point from which we can say—as one recent participant put it—"In Touchstones, I found my voice." In Stage 2, we must work to acknowledge that others also have voices. The goals of the second stage will therefore be to eliminate factions and subgroups, view each participant as someone who has something worth saying, and make each member of the group aware of his or her relationship to this process.

These goals will be achieved through continuing to analyze the discussions and considering the texts that explore ideas and issues that help us examine the reasons groups fragment into factions. In this second stage, we will begin to observe our own behavior and thinking and the ways in which our habits guide our actions for better or worse. We will see how our own entrenched desire for certainty and security leads us to evaluate the credibility of speakers. We will learn to recognize that all the members of the group are committed to self-examination, and therefore we will learn to respect them as legitimate speakers. We will then progress to the next stage, which is to learn to listen to what is said.

Stage 3: Listening and Understanding

The third stage is in certain respects the most difficult. In Stages 1 and 2, we explored how first professional credentials and then personal compatibility work to fragment the group. We saw that we first pay attention to those whom we consider experts and then to those whom we like. Now the difficulty we must overcome comes from a source deeper within ourselves. In the third stage, we must face and start to overcome the difference between hearing and listening. Simply hearing the sounds and words that strike us is not listening. Listening is an activity requiring skill and self-awareness.

Our experience of the world is often described as a compound of what we contribute and what the world presents. Our contribution is sometimes seen as a paradigm or model that we impose on the world and which, through its familiarity, helps us make sense of things. Without some source of structure through which to order the massive amounts of information that confront us daily, we would no doubt be overwhelmed and unable to function in the world. Various sources for these organizing and filtering structures include philosophical beliefs, language, culture, education, life experiences, and the epoch or period in history in which we live. Not only do we apply concepts on the world, we also impose them on other people. We create expectations for what others say, think, and do. We impose ourselves on what we hear. It is this trait that makes it so difficult to listen to others. We all make the thoughts and words of others into corollaries of our own thoughts, opinions, and attitudes. In the third stage of Mapping the Future, we attempt to face and overcome this tendency.

Facing the ways in which we impose our presuppositions and assumptions on others involves facing ourselves. We will see that facing ourselves can only be done with the help of others. However, we will not attempt to strip ourselves entirely of our preconceptions. Our preconceptions are so deep and pervasive that we could not simply surrender them even should we desire to do so. Instead our task in Stage 3 is to become more aware of these assumptions and the ways in which they shape our experience of the world.

In this stage, you will also notice a shift in the relationship of the components of the discussion process. Those components—our experience, the dynamics of the process, and the texts—are always present. However, in the first two stages, the texts are generally not as central as the other two components. In the third stage, the texts rise to equal prominence. In the very effort we make to understand a text, we will learn to listen to and understand one another. Although our discussions will never focus solely on textual interpretation, the text will begin to act as a touchstone for us. Exploring an unfamiliar and somewhat alien text helps us to prepare to listen to others and also to ourselves. This skill of listening in turn prepares us to join with others to participate fully in a discussion group.

Stage 4: Leadership, Participation, and Commitment

The examination of our own presuppositions in Stage 3 leads to the fourth and final stage. Stage 4 examines leadership based on our experience in discussion. In this stage, we will read texts that invite us to consider different aspects of the issues of leadership and participation, and we will intentionally practice and reflect on a new type of leadership.

This stage will be somewhat familiar. For instance, from the very start of the program, each group member will have participated in leadership tasks and issues to varying degrees. Throughout the units, everyone will have written questions to open discussions. And in every meeting, all members will have shared some responsibility with the leader for the success of the discussion. On a personal level, you also will have confronted leadership issues. You will have probably encountered times when you became frustrated with the direction of the conversation or by the dominance or hesitation of other group members. And you might have blamed the process or the leader or the text or the other participants for your frustration. But at some point, you will have probably asked what the group needs or how you could help the group get past a certain problem. Such a moment marks the point at which you will have moved from acting simply as a member of the group waiting for something to happen to acting in the context of the discussion process to determine the shape it will ultimately assume.

These experiences with leadership will crystallize in the fourth stage—the stage in which leadership will come to the forefront. With a small group, you will share responsibility not only for leading but also for designing a session. This stage will be the opportunity to use all the skills developed through the course of the program and to begin to recognize that in discussions, the needs of the individual and the responsibility toward the group need not conflict.

The cooperative leadership that emerges within the discussion group and that we consider explicitly in Stage 4 becomes the model for an attitude of responsibility and openness that enables profound change to take place. In Touchstones, participants actually have the important opportunity to watch this type of cooperative leadership emerge within the group. By its nature, any real change is disorienting. Our usual maps and landmarks no longer offer clear direction. The attempt to develop the cooperative thinking of shared leadership within the group might feel chaotic at first, such as when we find our usual ways of interacting challenged. We may be tempted to take refuge in the more familiar hierarchical ways of interacting. But in the same way that we watched form emerge in discussions that seemed to be without a rigid structure, we will eventually see direction emerge in our exploration and self-examination—a direction for which we will all feel some ownership and a success for which we will all take some responsibility.

Paired Texts as Touchstones

In each unit of this volume, we will use a pair of texts as tools to explore our assumptions. Each pair of texts addresses a question or topic of recognizably great importance in our lives. Examples include the following: When, if ever, should one break a law? What are the uses and dangers of technology? What is power? Just as a jeweler's touchstone is used to determine the identity of metals, these texts are used to reveal our unexamined opinions about these concerns. We will contrast those opinions that we hold entirely acceptable or true with those that are alien or false for us.

The first text of each pair is always a noncontemporary work, chosen because its general concern is recognizable but its approach and style are somewhat unfamiliar. It is distant in either time or culture, or in both. This distance of noncontemporary texts from us is what makes them valuable for discussion. The strangeness of the text invites the members of the group to submerge their personal differences and to cooperate in trying to understand what the text presents.

In the first unit, for example, the text from Saint Thomas Aquinas's Treatise on Law asks whether it is ever appropriate for an individual to break a law. Aquinas's treatment of the question, however, shows certain assumed opinions about law and nature that are no longer common. The group members have to restrain their differences about the question of the appropriateness of breaking a law to see how Aquinas's treatment of that question holds together. We discuss the issue by working together to understand it through Aquinas's eyes.

The second text of the unit is usually contemporary in the sense that it deals with an issue on the basis of opinions and conclusions we recognize. Most often, it is a text from our own time and culture. Of course, we might or might not share the opinions and conclusions evident in the text; however, because of our familiarity with these opinions and conclusions, they will evoke our active agreement or disagreement. This second text reintroduces the conditions for controversy that are present in our society and that were suspended within the first text. In our responses to the second text, our differences can be displayed, talked about, and thought about. Members of the group might not change their minds about the issue, but they will leave the discussion with a better appreciation for the basis of their opinions and of opinions with which they disagree.

The contemporary work in the first unit is a section of Martin Luther King Jr.'s "Letter from Birmingham Jail." In the letter, King sets forth the conditions for appropriate civil disobedience. Although King refers to Aquinas's work, the argument in his letter differs in important ways from Aquinas's treatise. King does not base his argument on a notion of nature like Aquinas's but rather on the effects of law on the human personality. He argues that we have a duty to disobey unjust laws in a peaceful and respectful way. There are many people who disagree with this point of view, many who agree, and many who aren't sure. More important, the group members will disagree about how to judge whether a law is unjust and, if so, whether proper means of disobedience exist. The juxtaposition of this text with the first, combined with the Touchstones Discussion format, will make thoughtful discussion of such important concerns possible.

Orientation Session:
Defining Expectations

Orientation Worksheet

1. What do you hope to gain from this discussion group? Rate each of the following choices on a scale of 1 to 10, with 10 indicating something you desire strongly and 1 indicating something you do not desire at all.

_____ Explore interesting texts and topics

_____ Clarify my own ideas

_____ Increase my communication skills

_____ Learn to be part of a discussion group

_____ Improve my listening skills

_____ Hear new perspectives

_____ Is there something else you would add to this list? Add it here and rate it on the same scale.

_____

2. What kinds of issues or problems do you think might arise in the group that would prevent the success of this activity?

3. *Mapping the Future* is organized around four stages of group development: (1) dealing with issues of authority and expertise; (2) learning to see every person as a legitimate speaker; (3) learning to listen and understand; and (4) learning to act simultaneously as a leader and a participant. Which stage do you expect to present the greatest challenges? Why?

4. Write a question to start a discussion on *Frankenstein*.

Frankenstein
by Mary Shelley

The creature that Dr. Frankenstein created has been living in the forest near a family whom he has come to admire greatly. He has been leaving them wood for their fire and generally attempting to assist them. In addition, he has been reading many books, such as Plutarch's Lives *and Milton's* Paradise Lost. *Finally he feels the pain of his isolation and resolves to make contact with the family.*

These were the reflections of my hours of despondency and solitude; but when I contemplated the virtues of the cottagers, their amiable and benevolent dispositions, I persuaded myself that when they should become acquainted with my admiration of their virtues they would compassionate me and overlook my personal deformity. Could they turn from their door one who, however monstrous, solicited their compassion and friendship? I resolved at least not to despair, but in every way to fit myself for an interview with them which would decide my fate. I postponed this attempt for some months longer, for the importance attached to its success inspired me with a dread lest I should fail. Besides, I found that my understanding improved so much with every day's experience that I was unwilling to commence this undertaking until a few more months should have added to my sagacity.

The winter advanced, and an entire revolution of the seasons had taken place since I awoke into life. My attention at this time was solely directed toward my plan of introducing myself into the cottage. I revolved many projects, but that on which I finally fixed was to enter the dwelling when the blind old man should be alone. I had sagacity enough to discover that the unnatural hideousness of my person was the chief object of horror to those who had formerly beheld me. My voice, although harsh, had nothing terrible in it; I thought, therefore, that if in the absence of his children I could gain the good will and mediation of the old De Lacey, I might by his means be tolerated by the younger.

My heart beat quick; this was the hour and moment of trial, which would decide my hopes or realize my fears. The servants were gone to a neighboring fair. All was silent in and around the cottage; it was an excellent opportunity. Yet, when I proceeded to execute my plan, my limbs failed me and I sank to the ground. Again I rose, and exerting all the firmness of which I was master, removed the planks that I had placed before my hovel to conceal my retreat. The fresh air revived me, and, with renewed determination, I approached the door of their cottage.

I knocked. "Who is there?" said the old man. "Come in."

I entered and sat down, and a silence ensued. I knew that every minute was precious to me, yet I remained irresolute in what manner to commence the interview, when the old man addressed me. "By your language, stranger, I suppose you are my countryman. Are you French?"

"No; but I was educated by a French family and understand that language only. I am now going to claim the protection of some friends, whom I sincerely love, and of whose favor I have some hopes."

"Are they Germans?"

"No, they are French. But let us change the subject. I am an unfortunate and deserted creature; I look around and I have no relation or friend upon earth. These amiable people to whom I go have never seen me and know little of me. I am full of fears, for if I fail there, I am an outcast in the world forever."

"Do not despair. To be friendless is indeed to be unfortunate, but the hearts of men, when unprejudiced by any obvious self-interest, are full of brotherly love and charity. Rely, therefore, on your hopes, and if these friends are good and amiable, do not despair."

"They are kind—they are the most excellent creatures in the world—but, unfortunately, they are prejudiced against me. I have good dispositions; my life has been hitherto harmless and in some degree beneficial; but a fatal prejudice clouds their eyes, and where they ought to see a feeling and kind friend, they behold a detestable monster."

"That is indeed unfortunate; but if you are really blameless, cannot you undeceive them? May I know the names and residence of those friends?"

I paused. This, I thought, was the moment of decision, which was to rob me of or bestow on me happiness forever. I struggled vainly for firmness sufficient to answer him, but the effort destroyed all my remaining strength. I sank on the chair and sobbed aloud. At that moment I heard the steps of my younger protectors. I had not a moment to lose, but seizing the hand of the old man, I cried, "Now is the time! Save and protect me! You and your family are the friends whom I seek. Do not desert me in the hour of trial!"

"Great God!" exclaimed the old man. "Who are you?"

At that instant the cottage door was opened, and Felix, Sofia, and Agatha entered. Who can describe their horror and consternation on beholding me? Agatha fainted, and Sofia, unable to attend her friend, rushed out of the cottage. Felix darted forward, and with supernatural force tore me from his father, to whose knees I clung; in a transport of fury, he dashed me to the ground and struck me violently with a stick. I could have torn him limb from limb, as the lion rends the antelope. But my heart sank within me as with bitter sickness, and I refrained. I saw him on the point of repeating his blow, when, overcome by pain and anguish, I quitted the cottage, and in the general tumult escaped unperceived to my hovel.

Cursed, cursed creator! Why did I live? Why, in that instant, did I not extinguish the spark of existence that you had so wantonly bestowed? I know not; despair had not yet taken possession of me; my feelings were those of rage and revenge. I could with pleasure have destroyed the cottage and its inhabitants and have glutted myself with their shrieks and misery.

When night came, I quitted my retreat and wandered in the wood; and now, no longer restrained by the fear of discovery, I gave vent to my anguish in fearful howlings. I was like a wild beast that had broken the toils, destroying the objects that obstructed me and ranging through the wood with a stag-like swiftness. Oh! What a miserable night I passed! The cold stars shone in mockery, and the bare trees waved their branches above me; now and then the sweet voice of a bird burst forth amidst the universal stillness. All, save I, were at rest or in enjoyment. I, like the arch-fiend, bore a hell within me, and finding myself unsympathized with, wished to tear up the trees, spread havoc and destruction around me, and then to have sat down and enjoyed the ruin.

The sun rose; I heard the voices of men and knew that it was impossible to return to my retreat during that day. Accordingly, I hid myself in some thick underwood, determining to devote the ensuing hours to reflection on my situation.

Presently two countrymen passed by, but pausing near the cottage, they entered into conversation, using violent gesticulations; but I did not understand what they said, as they spoke the language of the country, which differed from that of my protectors. Soon after, however, Felix approached with another man; I was surprised, as I knew that he had not quitted the cottage that morning, and waited anxiously to discover from his discourse the meaning of these unusual appearances.

"Do you consider," said his companion to him, "that you will be obliged to pay three months' rent and to lose the produce of your garden? I do not wish to take any unfair advantage, and I beg therefore that you will take some days to consider of your determination."

"It is utterly useless," replied Felix, "we can never again inhabit your cottage. The life of my father is in the greatest danger, owing to the dreadful circumstances that I have related. My wife and my sister will never recover from their horror. I entreat you not to reason with me any more. Take possession of your tenement and let me fly from this place."

Felix trembled violently as he said this. He and his companion entered the cottage, in which they remained for a few minutes, and then departed. I never more saw any of the family of De Lacey.

I continued for the remainder of the day in my hovel in a state of utter and stupid despair. My protectors had departed and had broken the only link that held me to the world. For the first time, the feelings of revenge and hatred filled my bosom and I did not strive to control them, but allowing myself to be borne away by the stream, I bent my mind toward injury and death. When I thought of my friends, of the mild voice of De Lacey, the gentle eyes of Agatha, and the exquisite beauty of the Arabian, these thoughts vanished and a gush of tears somewhat soothed me. But again when I reflected that they had spurned and deserted me, anger returned, a rage of anger, and unable to injure anything human, I turned my fury toward inanimate objects. As night advanced I placed a variety of combustibles around the cottage. I lighted the dry branch of a tree and danced with fury around the devoted cottage, my eyes fixed on the western horizon, the edge of which the moon nearly touched. The wind fanned the fire, and the cottage was quickly enveloped by the flames, which clung to it and licked it with their forked and destroying tongues.

As soon as I was convinced that no assistance could save any part of the habitation, I quitted the scene and sought for refuge in the woods.

Stage 1
Authority and Expertise

Rules and Laws

Almost every one of our actions is directly or indirectly connected with rules and laws. There are the laws of our country, the rules of behavior in an organization like a university or a corporation, the rules of a game, the rules that we establish with one another in families or among friends, and many others. In a world in which we increasingly feel diversity must be encouraged and respected, we require ever more complex rules to allow the internal rules of various cultures to coexist.

Many of these rules, such as the "No Smoking" signs that we so often see in public areas, are explicit. Others are so ingrained that we rarely notice them because they have become a part of us. For example, we instinctively know that certain foods are eaten with or without certain utensils—we use our hands to eat a candy bar or chips, but a fork to eat a salad. These kinds of rules are usually only recognized when we are surprised to see someone break one of them. Some rules and laws are necessary, others are useful, and others seem superfluous. Some rules and laws appear arbitrary, others seem to be based on some thought and appear reasonable. Some laws seem just to us whereas other laws appear entirely unjust. All societies we know of have a code of behavior or a set of laws, and scientists have even tried to uncover the rules that govern societies of animals.

A class in a school or university also has rules. In lecture classes, attendees are expected to sit quietly facing the front of the room while the professor speaks. Attendees are also expected to ask questions at the appropriate time and in the appropriate way—perhaps by raising a hand and being acknowledged. In such a situation, all the rules reinforce the purpose of that type of activity. The premise of a lecture class or a presentation at a place of work is that the expert who has mastered a subject will convey his or her excitement and knowledge about the material. The format that you will experience here is different. It will be a seminar or a discussion. The purposes of a discussion are different from those of a lecture, but there are still rules established to achieve those purposes.

What is a discussion? It is a format that assumes equality among participants. Each discussion will have a leader, but the leader will play a different role from the one a teacher or professor plays in a lecture class. The discussion leader will not be an expert there to entertain, amuse, or impart information. The leader's role instead is to engage the entire group in a cooperative exploration—of a topic or texts—in which each person's opinion is respected. The texts to be read will raise issues that do not have a single correct response. Instead, answers will generally be better or worse rather than correct or incorrect. There is diversity in every collection of people and, if our discussions are to achieve real richness and depth, each person's voice must be acknowledged. Such discussions require some ground rules. We propose five of them:

1. Read the text carefully.
2. Listen to what others say, and don't interrupt.
3. Speak clearly.
4. Speak to all the members of the group.
5. Give others your respect.

These are the rules we will use to get started. However, it will take time and effort to act according to these rules and even longer until they feel natural. You might think that, because of particular circumstances, your group requires other rules in addition to these; or you may feel that some of these rules need to be suspended for brief periods if our goals are to be achieved. The rules are present to assist us in achieving our goals and may need to be modified, expanded, or adjusted. After each session, you will evaluate the successes and problems in that meeting. The evaluations will enable us at appropriate times to reflect on our progress, on how well we are adhering to our framework of rules, and on whether we need to create new rules. The two texts in this unit will help us focus on the issue of rules and laws. Saint Thomas Aquinas and Martin Luther King Jr. both consider when it is appropriate to break an unjust law. In dealing with this issue, they also define what a just law is and its relation to a law that we are either allowed to change or encouraged to violate or, in even more extreme cases, that we may be obligated to break.

Worksheet 1

The introduction to this session opens the topic of the role of rules and laws in all our lives. The texts consider the question of what might make a law unjust and what our reaction to such a law should be. The worksheet asks us to think about our own responses to the ground rules that will shape our discussions in Touchstones and to consider ways in which the rules of a discussion might be just or unjust.

1. Listed below are the ground rules we will follow in Touchstones Discussions.

    1. Read the text carefully.
    2. Listen to what others say, and don't interrupt.
    3. Speak clearly.
    4. Speak to all the members of the group.
    5. Give others your respect.

    Which ground rule will you find the most difficult to follow? Why?

2. Write another possible ground rule. What would the new rule help achieve?

3. After reading the texts, write a question that you would like the group to discuss.

Summa Theologica
by Saint Thomas Aquinas

Laws made by men are either just or unjust. If they are just, they rule our conscience because just laws are derived from the eternal law of God. As it says in Proverbs in the Bible, "By Me kings rule, and lawgivers decree just things." Laws are considered just on account of the purpose they serve, the authority of the lawgiver, and their form. They are just when the purpose is the common good, when the lawgiver does not exceed his right to make certain kinds of laws, and when the form of the laws places burdens on the subjects proportionate to their position in society. This last condition is true because since each man is a part of the community, each, in all that he is and has, belongs to the community. On the other hand, laws may be unjust in two ways. First, a law may be contrary to human good, through being opposed to the things we have just mentioned. In respect to the goal or purpose, an authority might impose burdensome laws on his subjects, which are not for the common good but rather the rulers' own selfish ends. Or a ruler might make a law that goes beyond the power committed to him. Or a law in its form may look toward the common good but not impose burdens that have a due proportion to the positions of the subjects within the community. All these are acts of violence rather than laws. Secondly, laws can be unjust through being opposed to the divine good. Such would be laws by tyrants forcing idolatry or anything else contrary to the divine law. Laws of this sort must never be followed. As is stated in the Acts of the Apostles, "We ought to obey God rather than men."

There are a number of objections that could be made to what has just been said.

The first objection is that a human law never binds a man's conscience because an inferior power cannot impose its law on the judgment of a higher power. But the power of man, which makes human law, is beneath divine power. Therefore human law cannot impose itself on the judgment of our consciences, which is based on divine law. To this I reply: The apostle Paul says in Romans that all human power is from God. "Therefore he who resists the power in matters that are within its scope resists the commands of God." So, such a person becomes guilty in his conscience.

The second objection is the following: The judgment made by our conscience depends primarily on the commandments of God. But sometimes the commandments of God are made void by human laws. Therefore, human law does not bind our consciences. I reply that this argument is true of laws that are contrary to God's commandments, for these commandments are beyond the scope of human power. In such matters, human law should not be obeyed.

There is also a third objection. Human laws often bring to men both injury and a loss of character. For according to Isaiah, "Shame on you who make unjust laws and burdensome decrees. You deprive the poor of justice and rob the weakest of my people of their rights." Since it is lawful for all to avoid oppression and violence, therefore human laws do not bind our conscience. I reply that this argument is true of any law that imposes an unjust burden on its subjects. The power that man holds from God does not extend to this. So, in such matters, a man is not bound to obey the law provided he can avoid causing scandal or inflicting an even worse injury by his disobedience.

When considering these matters another question arises. Should a human law be changed whenever a better law comes along? I answer that human law is rightly changed when such a change helps attain the common good. But, to a certain extent, the change of any law, even an unjust law, harms the common good. This is because custom helps a great deal in getting us to observe all laws. We can see this by noticing that anything that is done contrary to our usual customs, even in small matters, is looked at as a serious offense. So when any law is changed, the power of law itself is diminished in so far as a custom is abolished. Therefore, human law should never be changed, unless, in some way or other, the common good is compensated according to the extent of the harm done by breaking our habit of obeying laws. As the great legal thinker Gratian says, "In making a new law, one must have evidence of the benefits which will be derived before changing a law which has, for a long time, been considered just."

Letter from Birmingham Jail
by Martin Luther King Jr.

You express a great deal of anxiety over our willingness to break laws. This is certainly a legitimate concern. Since we so diligently urge people to obey the Supreme Court's decision of 1954 outlawing segregation in the public schools, at first glance it may seem rather paradoxical for us consciously to break laws. One may well ask: "How can you advocate breaking some laws and obeying others?" The answer lies in the fact that there are two types of laws: just and unjust. I would be the first to advocate obeying just laws. One has not only a legal but also a moral responsibility to obey laws. Conversely, one has a moral responsibility to disobey unjust laws. I would agree with Saint Augustine that "an unjust law is not law at all."

Now, what is the difference between the two? How does one determine whether a law is just or unjust? A just law is a man-made code that squares with the moral law or the law of God. An unjust law is a code that is out of harmony with the moral law. To put it in the terms of Saint Thomas Aquinas: An unjust law is a human law that is not rooted in eternal law and natural law. Any law that uplifts human personality is just. Any law that degrades human personality is unjust. All segregation statutes are unjust because segregation distorts the soul and damages the personality. It gives the segregator a false sense of superiority and the segregated a false sense of inferiority. Hence segregation is not only politically, economically, and sociologically unsound, it is morally wrong and sinful. Thus it is that I can urge men to obey the 1954 decision of the Supreme Court, for it is morally right, and I can urge them to disobey segregation ordinances, for they are morally wrong.

Let us consider a more concrete example of just and unjust laws. An unjust law is a code that a numerical or power majority group compels a minority group to obey but does not make binding on itself. This is difference made legal. By the same token, a just law is a code that a majority compels a minority to follow and that it is willing to follow itself. This is sameness made legal.

Let me give another explanation. A law is unjust if it is inflicted on a minority that, as a result of being denied the right to vote, had no part in enacting or devising the law. Who can say that the legislature of Alabama that set up that state's segregation laws was democratically elected? Throughout Alabama, all sorts of devious methods are used to prevent Negroes from becoming registered voters, and there are some counties in which, even though Negroes constitute a majority of the population, not a single Negro is registered. Can any law enacted under such circumstances be considered democratically structured?

Sometimes a law is just on its face and unjust in its application. For instance, I have been arrested on a charge of parading without a permit. Now, there is nothing wrong in having an ordinance that requires a permit for a parade. But such an ordinance becomes unjust when it is used to maintain segregation and to deny citizens the First Amendment privilege of peaceful assembly and protest.

I hope you are able to see the distinction I am trying to point out. In no sense do I advocate evading or defying the law, as would the rabid segregationist. That would lead to anarchy. One who breaks an unjust law must do so openly, lovingly, and with a willingness to accept the penalty.

Of course, there is nothing new about this kind of civil disobedience. It was practiced superbly by the early Christians, who were willing to face hungry lions and the excruciating pain of chopping blocks rather than submit to certain unjust laws of the Roman Empire. To a degree, academic freedom is a reality today because Socrates practiced civil disobedience. In our own nation, the Boston Tea Party represented a massive act of civil disobedience.

We should never forget that everything Adolf Hitler did in Germany was "legal" and everything the Hungarian freedom fighters did in Hungary was "illegal." It was "illegal" to aid and comfort a Jew in Hitler's Germany. Even so, I am sure that, had I lived in Germany at the time, I would have aided and comforted my Jewish brothers. If today I lived in a Communist country where certain principles dear to the Christian faith are suppressed, I would openly advocate disobeying that country's antireligious laws.

Discussion Evaluation Form

The items below are discussion dynamics that may or may not be present in your group. Decide to what extent you think that each dynamic was present in the discussion. Then decide whether you think the group needs to work to improve in this area.

	None Some Great deal	Need to Improve?
Dominance by some individuals	1 2 3 4 5 6 7 8 9 10	Yes ❑ No ❑
Cooperation	1 2 3 4 5 6 7 8 9 10	Yes ❑ No ❑
Silence	1 2 3 4 5 6 7 8 9 10	Yes ❑ No ❑
Interrupting	1 2 3 4 5 6 7 8 9 10	Yes ❑ No ❑
Respect	1 2 3 4 5 6 7 8 9 10	Yes ❑ No ❑
Balanced participation	1 2 3 4 5 6 7 8 9 10	Yes ❑ No ❑
Active listening	1 2 3 4 5 6 7 8 9 10	Yes ❑ No ❑
Lack of interest	1 2 3 4 5 6 7 8 9 10	Yes ❑ No ❑
Asking one other questions	1 2 3 4 5 6 7 8 9 10	Yes ❑ No ❑
Building on one other's contributions	1 2 3 4 5 6 7 8 9 10	Yes ❑ No ❑
Many people talking at once	1 2 3 4 5 6 7 8 9 10	Yes ❑ No ❑

Pick one of the dynamics that you think the group should work to improve, and explain why.

How would you rate this discussion on a scale of 1–10? _____

Questions, Power, and Authority

The questions teachers ask of us during our years in school generally have a very specific answer—a correct answer. The teacher is the authority on a specific subject matter, and these questions are often asked to test our understanding of the material. The teacher has the power to decide the worth of our answers and to determine a grade for our performance. In such classes, the teacher is the locus of power because he or she is the authority on both what we are to learn and whether we are learning it. The Touchstones Discussion sessions that we are undertaking are quite different. Although each session will have a leader who will take ultimate responsibility for the discussion process itself, he or she will in no way be an expert on the content discussed.

A Touchstones Discussion starts with a question. However, this question rarely has a single correct answer. It instead serves as the starting point for our exploration. Each participant will come to the meeting with at least one question for the group to discuss. Even though the leader's question will open the sessions in the initial stages, the group members will often be asked to read their questions aloud. This is important for many reasons, but especially because it enables each participant to hear other perspectives and the diversity of questions. Eventually, questions from the participants other than the leader will open the discussions.

Although the opening question initiates the discussion, it is not the only topic that will be discussed. It might not even be the most important question that could be raised about an issue or text. It is a starting point, and the interests of the group and the direction of the exploration might lead the discussion very far from where it began. However, the opening question is not arbitrary. It invites the group members to consider the opinions in the text, the relationship of the ideas raised in the text to the evolution of the group, or the connection of these issues with each individual's experience. The question, along with the text, sets the stage for the discussion but does not control its direction. It is the start of a path, one of many.

Opening questions can come in many varieties. In regard to the texts we considered in Unit 1, we could ask about (1) Aquinas's or King's view of an unjust law, (2) our thoughts about unjust laws, or (3) our attitudes toward, or our experiences with, unjust laws or rules in our society. The first question would generally lead to a textual discussion; the second would often lead to an abstract discussion that could be related to, or independent of, the text; and the third would likely lead to a personal account of particular experiences. Each of these approaches can be useful for an initiating question. However, each also has disadvantages as a starting point for discussion. A textual question like the first can lead to an academic consideration of the issue, or it could encourage the members of the group to make professorial statements about what they imagine King or Aquinas believed. Conceptual questions like the second one can frequently lead to categorical assertions of opinions without any exploration or inquiry. Experiential questions like the third one encourage anecdotal accounts that can either entertain or bore the group, thus leaving members other than the speaker passive.

The most fertile questions have potential to pass from one type of consideration to another—for instance, from the texts to our experiences and back again. As you formulate a question, keep in mind that you can also draw on the group's experience as a group or on your common experience of discussion dynamics. A good question most often tries to touch on more than one of these three focal points—the text, the interests of the group, and your group's shared history. Although there is no such thing as a perfect opening question, the following few criteria can help ensure a good question:

- The question should be short and simple. Make sure there is no need to write it down for it to be remembered and understood.

- One's first strong response to a text is often the best source for an opening question. Although different people will often have different questions, similar questions occur quite often. You should not view creating your question as a contest in originality.

- Your question should be one that is genuinely a question for you. This does not mean you have no opinion about the answer, but that you are willing to change your mind about that answer and are eager to hear the thoughts of others.

Most important, remember that the initiating question is not an assertion of your power or authority, but an invitation. At this moment in the process, the leader is like a good host whose concern is the needs and interests of the guest. In the seminars you attended in the past, the leader's questions probably set the stage and direction for the discussion. Such seminars are often not genuine discussions but more similar to traditional forms of educational experiences. In genuine discussions, power will not be lodged in the opening question but rather the collaborative exploration of the group. The leader will be given authority as the conscience of the group—keeping everyone on task and responsible to the ground rules, the timeline, and the texts. The two texts for this unit deal explicitly with power—what it means to have it, why people desire it, and whether it is the force that underlies all our actions. Plato and Nietzsche present two versions of the traditional view of power and enable us to start to explore both their plausibility and their attraction for us.

Worksheet 2

Both texts for this session are about power. Plato explores the power that the strong exercise over the weak, and Nietzsche conceives of power as the motivating force for all of life. In the introduction, we considered the role and authority of the leader of a discussion and the power that is exercised in asking the opening question. The worksheet asks us to think about other situations in which power is exercised over others and how the ways in which it is employed may affect outcomes.

1. The items below describe people who exercise power and authority in a particular leadership situation. Rank the form of leadership you believe to be most typically employed in the described situation on a scale of 1 to 10, with 10 being the most authoritarian leadership and 1 being the most shared leadership. Then think about the advantages and disadvantages of that style of leadership for achieving the stated goal. For example, a teacher's goal may be to interest students in a subject, and a teacher teaching in a traditional way might be rated as an 8 or 9. One advantage of this style of teaching might be that a lively and entertaining teacher may succeed in focusing students' attention. One disadvantage could be that the students are likely to remain passive and might not internalize that interest. For each item below, you are also asked to say what you would consider an ideal form of leadership for achieving the stated goal. You might, for example, think that a teacher would be more successful as a 6 or 7 rather than an 8 or 9, because some sharing of power with students would increase their motivation and initiative.

    a) Doctor leading a team of nurses

        Goal: To restore a seriously ill patient to health

        Leadership style: _____ typical _____ ideal

        Advantage of actual style:

        Disadvantage of actual style:

    b) A general leading a staff

        Goal: To plan (not conduct) a military campaign

        Leadership style: _____ typical _____ ideal

        Advantage of actual style:

        Disadvantage of actual style:

c) A principal leading a staff of teachers

Goal: To improve students' performance on tests

Leadership style:_____ typical _____ ideal

Advantage of actual style:

Disadvantage of actual style:

d) A basketball coach leading a team

Goal: To win the championship

Leadership style:_____ typical _____ ideal

Advantage of actual style:

Disadvantage of actual style:

e) A parent raising children

Goal: To get a child to assist in household tasks

Leadership style:_____ typical _____ ideal

Advantage of actual style:

Disadvantage of actual style:

2. After reading the texts, write a possible opening question for the discussion.

The Republic: Book I
by Plato

[Socrates, Thrasymachus, and some others have been discussing the nature of justice. Thrasymachus is sure he has a very good answer to the question of what justice is, and begins to speak.]

Thrasymachus: Now listen! Justice is nothing other than what is beneficial for those who rule.

Socrates: Tell me more clearly what you mean, Thrasymachus.

Thrasymachus: Don't you know that some states are ruled democratically, others by a group of aristocrats, and still others by a tyrant?

Socrates: Yes, I do.

Thrasymachus: And each ruling group makes laws for its own benefit. A tyrant makes tyrannical laws, a democracy makes democratic laws, and so on. By making such laws, and so determining what is just, the rulers declare that their own advantage is also justice for those who are ruled. Whoever does not act for the advantage of the rulers becomes a lawbreaker and unjust. So, this is what I mean: In every state justice is whatever is beneficial for the established ruling body, for those who have power.

Socrates: Are the rulers of states perfect, or do they make mistakes?

Thrasymachus: Of course, they sometimes make mistakes.

Socrates: So, when they make laws, they sometimes do this incorrectly. That is, they make laws that, in fact, are not beneficial to themselves.

Thrasymachus: I suppose so.

Socrates: But, according to you, justice always means obeying the rulers.

Thrasymachus: Of course.

Socrates: Then, according to you, justice is not only doing what is beneficial for the rulers, but also sometimes doing what is not beneficial for them.

Thrasymachus: Not at all. Do you suppose that I call someone a ruler, someone who is stronger and more powerful, at the moment he is making a mistake?

Socrates: As a matter of fact, I did.

Thrasymachus: That's because you like to twist what someone is saying. Take an example. If a doctor makes a mistake about a patient, do you call him a doctor because of his mistake? Of course not. In the same way, rulers who really are rulers do not make mistakes. When they are making mistakes, they are not really rulers. So, what I said is true. Justice is whatever benefits the rulers, that is, those who are the powerful and stronger.

Socrates: I am not trying to twist your words, Thrasymachus. Let's get back to the argument. Is the doctor you were just talking about primarily someone who cares for the sick or someone who makes money? I mean the man who really is a doctor.

Thrasymachus: He is someone who cares for the sick, of course.

Socrates: And what about the captain of a ship? Is he someone who rules over passengers and crew, or is he merely another sailor?

Thrasymachus: He is a ruler, of course.

Socrates: Do the doctor and the captain seek their own benefit, or the benefit of those in their care?

Thrasymachus: Of those in their care.

Socrates: Isn't the same true of anyone who holds a position of authority and knows what he is doing? In other words, such a person looks to the benefit of those over whom he has authority and not to his own benefit. This is what it really means to be a ruler.

Thrasymachus: Socrates, you should stop sniveling like a child so much.

Socrates: Why do you say that?

Thrasymachus: Because you are naive enough to think that shepherds take care of sheep for the sake of the sheep, and not for their own profit, and that rulers in states think of anything but their own benefit. You don't understand that justice really benefits the powerful man who rules, but does not benefit the weak man who serves and obeys. The weak man who acts justly benefits the strong whom he obeys. The powerful man who acts unjustly benefits himself. Everywhere you turn, Socrates, the just man has less than the unjust man. When a just man and an unjust man make a contract, the unjust man gets the better deal. When there are taxes to be paid, the unjust man pays less, and when there are profits to be distributed, the unjust man gets more. When a just man holds public office, his private affairs suffer from neglect. He gets no benefit from his position, and his friends and relatives are mad at him because he won't do them any favors. The situation of the unjust man is the opposite of this in all respects. I am talking about the man who is unjust in a grand way. When someone who is unjust in a small way (say, by being a burglar, kidnapper, or thief) gets caught, he is punished and made to suffer public humiliation. But when someone is unjust in a grand way, by being a dictator for example, he is not punished, but called happy and powerful and strong. The people over whom he rules call him this as does anyone else who hears about him. So, Socrates, when a man is unjust on a big enough scale, he is stronger, freer, more powerful, and more of a man than the just man. So what I said in the beginning is true. Just actions benefit the powerful man who rules and is himself unjust.

Socrates: Thrasymachus, this is quite an amazing argument you've made. Please don't go away before we've had a chance to find out whether it is true or not. This is not a small matter. The lives we lead depend on the truth or falsity of what you have said.

The Will to Power
by Friedrich Nietzsche

The will to power, the desire for power, is the most fundamental stimulus to action. All other stimuli are only outgrowths and developments of this. We are told that every living thing is supposed to be striving after happiness or pleasure. It is truer and more interesting to think of each of us striving for power. "There is a striving for power, or rather for an increase of power." All driving force is the will to power. There is no other physical or psychic force except this. It can be shown most clearly that every living thing does everything it can, not to preserve itself, but to become more, to become greater and more powerful.

The will to accumulate force is special to life, society, state, custom, and authority. Should we not also be permitted to assume this will as a cause in chemistry and in the cosmic order? The only reality is the will to grow stronger. The fundamental law of things is not self-preservation or the conservation of energy, as our science supposes, but the will to take, dominate, increase, and grow stronger.

Life, as the form of being most familiar to us, is specifically a will to the accumulation of power. All the processes of life depend on this. Life strives after a maximal feeling of power. It is essentially a striving for more power. All striving and desire is nothing other than this striving for power.

If pleasure accompanies every increase of power, and displeasure emerges from every failure to dominate or resist, one might ask if we should not rather assume pleasure and displeasure as the chief facts instead of the will to power. Is will possible without these two? But remember, we can always ask, who feels pleasure and who wants power? This would be an absurd question if the essence itself were feelings of pleasure and displeasure instead of the will that feels the pleasure, the will to power. Opposites and obstacles are necessary for the will to power. The possibility of failure must grow with the strength of the resistance that a force seeks to master. Since a force can act only on what resists it, there is necessarily an element of displeasure in every action. However, this displeasure acts as a lure of life and strengthens the will to power. It is not the satisfaction of the will that causes pleasure but rather the will's forward thrust toward becoming master over that which stands in its way. The feeling of pleasure lies precisely in the dissatisfaction of the will. In fact, the will is never satisfied unless it has opponents and resistance. "The happy man, the contented man" is the ideal of a herd animal.

Growth is part of the concept of life. Life must extend its power and consequently incorporate alien forces. When drugged by the narcotic of morality, one speaks instead of an individual's right to defend himself. One might, as easily, speak of his right to attack. Both, and attack more than defense, are necessary to every living thing. Aggressive and defensive self-interest are not matters of choice or right. They are the necessities of life itself.

The same holds true whether one considers an individual or a society. A society's right to punish others, or to defend itself, is improperly called a "right." Rights are acquired through treaties. But self-protection and self-defense do not rest on the basis of a treaty. These are not mere rights but rest on the same basis as the other crucial need of a society. This other crucial need is its need to conquer its lust for power, whether by arms, trade, commerce, or colonization. It makes as much sense to call all these needs "rights," as it would to view growth as a right. A right to growth! A society that definitely and instinctively abandons war and conquest is in decline. It is ripe for democracy and the rule of shopkeepers.

Discussion Evaluation Form

The items below are discussion dynamics that may or may not be present in your group. Decide to what extent you think that each dynamic was present in the discussion. Then decide whether you think the group needs to work to improve in this area.

	None Some Great deal	Need to Improve?
Dominance by some individuals	1 2 3 4 5 6 7 8 9 10	Yes ❏ No ❏
Cooperation	1 2 3 4 5 6 7 8 9 10	Yes ❏ No ❏
Silence	1 2 3 4 5 6 7 8 9 10	Yes ❏ No ❏
Interrupting	1 2 3 4 5 6 7 8 9 10	Yes ❏ No ❏
Respect	1 2 3 4 5 6 7 8 9 10	Yes ❏ No ❏
Balanced participation	1 2 3 4 5 6 7 8 9 10	Yes ❏ No ❏
Active listening	1 2 3 4 5 6 7 8 9 10	Yes ❏ No ❏
Lack of interest	1 2 3 4 5 6 7 8 9 10	Yes ❏ No ❏
Asking one other questions	1 2 3 4 5 6 7 8 9 10	Yes ❏ No ❏
Building on one other's contributions	1 2 3 4 5 6 7 8 9 10	Yes ❏ No ❏
Many people talking at once	1 2 3 4 5 6 7 8 9 10	Yes ❏ No ❏

Pick one of the dynamics that you think the group should work to improve, and explain why.

How would you rate this discussion on a scale of 1–10? _____

Experts and Expertise

One need only look through the yellow pages of the local telephone directory to see how many experts and forms of expertise exist. We are so used to this quantity that we are rarely surprised by it. Our society is so filled with experts, and this fact so shapes the way we view one another, that often the first thing we ask a new acquaintance is "What do you do?" Our expectations concerning expertise are particularly important to bring to the surface when forming a discussion group. This step is important because expertise often determines for us who has the right to speak in certain situations and about certain topics. The possibility of genuine discussion, however, depends on our ability to speak with one another without the type of expertise that we associate with professional credentials.

What, then, is the specific expertise and role of a discussion leader? The discussion leader should be focused on allowing and encouraging others to share the leadership. The leader's role is to be the conscience of the group. The leader seeks to inculcate in each group member a sense of responsibility for the well being of the group as a whole. This is a gradual process. For it to take place, our habits and expectations, and the presuppositions that support them, must be scrutinized and modified. Eventually, each member of the group should in every session be thinking both as a leader and as a participant. Making this possible is the leader's task, although the leader cannot guarantee that it will occur. In each situation, the leader must balance the short-term need to address particular problems that are blocking discussion with the long-term goal of the group taking responsibility for the success of the discussion.

The omnipresence of experts in our culture makes it difficult for us to realize that many societies are not filled with experts. Certainly, in most societies we know about, there are some forms of expertise that bestow authority and power. The making of weapons, the relationship between humans and gods or spirits, and the treatment of diseases are often fields in which some members of a society have special knowledge or skill. However, although these crafts require a special sort of knowledge, it is not always the case that the yellow pages of another culture would list such categories. Often, this knowledge is a function of age, or rather of the expected experience that comes with age. In such situations, moving from the status of one who does not know to that of one who does becomes a rite of initiation. In some societies, every normal adult might be a weapon maker, healer, priest, and potential ruler once a certain age or status is achieved.

Although some form of expertise perhaps characterizes all societies, it is the emergence of science, technology, and modern forms of production that have extensively multiplied reliance on expertise. Both science and mass production recognize nothing as, at least in principle, outside their scope. The progress of science and technology suggests to some thinkers that all functions of our society will continue to be compartmentalized into areas of expertise. It is certainly not clear that the more ancient categories of wisdom and craft can or should be revived; that is one of the issues we will explore through our discussions. But it is also not clear that the claims of science and technology to universal applicability are anything more than an instance of such experts' own will to power. In the progress of our Touchstones Discussions, we might be creating a hybrid way of approaching the world that merges the technical expertise associated with science and technology and the deep experience of life that constitutes wisdom.

The worksheet for this meeting will ask us to explore our intuitions about expertise: On what topics would we accept expert advice? For what topics might we think that the claim that there are experts is misleading and deprives us of the right to decide for ourselves? Both texts further shed light on expertise in that they connect mathematics and science with other concerns about philosophy, virtue, and the general search for truth. We will see that discussing these connections does not require us to become professionals on these subjects but rather requires that we should not see the subjects as the exclusive concern of professionals.

Worksheet 3

The introduction to this unit raises the issue of expertise and the importance attached to it in our culture. Readings related to the fields of mathematics and science are effective for bringing this issue to the surface because these are subjects in which technical expertise is particularly valued, and in which those of us who lack this expertise may feel most intimidated and inclined to defer to experts. However, our particular selections from Nicomachus of Gerasa and Henri Poincaré—by asking questions relating mathematics to other areas of our experience—help create an environment in which experts and nonexperts can discuss these subjects seriously with one another. To get us started thinking about our perspectives on expertise, the worksheet helps us examine the areas in which we would seek advice from someone with expertise, and the areas in which we would want to make our own decisions.

1. For each of the items below, consider whether you would seek to be guided by another person and, if so, on what basis you would choose that person. Choose from among the following options, and write the corresponding number in the blank for each item.

   1. A person who knows me and has my best interests in mind.
   2. A person with a rare talent in this area.
   3. A person with an advanced degree in this area.
   4. A person with a great deal of experience in this sort of situation.
   5. I would not choose to seek advice from another.

   _____ a) What color to paint your bedroom
   _____ b) What career to choose
   _____ c) Whether to marry a specific person
   _____ d) Why you are feeling a pain in your stomach
   _____ e) Whether to invest in a certain stock
   _____ f) Why you are depressed
   _____ g) What religion, if any, to adhere to
   _____ h) Whether to place an elderly parent in a retirement home
   _____ i) What computer to purchase
   _____ j) What to serve to important guests whom you don't know
   _____ k) Whether to support the cloning of human embryos for purposes of medical research

2. For one of the above, briefly explain the reason for your response.

3. After reading the texts, write an opening question for the discussion.

Introduction to Arithmetic
by Nicomachus of Gerasa

Science and philosophy were first made systematic under the leadership of Pythagoras, and this thinker defined philosophy as the love of wisdom. Before Pythagoras, all people who had any definite knowledge were considered wise men; for example a carpenter, a shoemaker, or a navigator. Pythagoras limited the title of wise man to those who knew and understood what was truly real. The desire and pursuit of this knowledge, which he considered the only thing worth knowing, he called philosophy.

The wisdom which philosophers strive after concerns those things that are truly real. These are the things that last forever and remain the same. The truly real things are not bodily, material objects, for material objects are forever involved in a continuous flow and change. Instead, the truly real things are the immaterial things which, when they first appear to us in bodies, appear as qualities, quantities, sizes, equalities, times, and places. Of themselves, all these are unchangeable. The bodies in which we first see them certainly get larger and smaller, become equal and unequal, become more or less. But bigness, equality, and numbers by themselves do not change. Philosophy concerns itself with what they are like by themselves. There are four sciences that deal with these eternal things: arithmetic, geometry, astronomy, and music theory. Our question is, which of these four sciences is most important for us to learn as philosophers?

Evidently, the science that naturally exists before the others is superior and is the origin, root, or, as it were, the mother of the others. This most superior science we call arithmetic. Arithmetic is naturally prior in birth because the other sciences require it, but arithmetic does not require them. If arithmetic is abolished, geometry, music theory, and astronomy are also abolished. But if they are abolished, arithmetic can still exist. What is meant by abolished can be seen from the following example. "Animal" comes naturally before "man." Abolish "man" and there can still be "animal"; abolish "animal" and you also abolish "man." So it is with arithmetic in relation to geometry, music, and astronomy. For example, if geometry exists, arithmetic is necessarily implied. For if we speak of three- or four-sided figures, the numbers 3 and 4 must previously exist. But the numbers 3 and 4 can exist without there being any three- and four-sided figures. Geometry implies arithmetic, but arithmetic does not imply geometry. Everything that nature has ordered in the universe seems to have been systematically determined and ordered in accordance with number. This came about through the forethought and mind of Him that created all things. The pattern of the universe was fixed, like a preliminary sketch, by the rule of number in the mind of the world-creating God. The idea of number is the true and eternal essence of number, and with reference to it, as to an artistic plan, all things like time, motion, the heavens, and the stars have been created. The numbers that we discover in bodies, in time, in motion, and in the stars are not the thought of number in the mind of the world creator, but yet they did all emerge from that thought.

Like the divine thought, each number is a unity, but like the flowing and changing bodies that are counted, the numbers are many. And each number we discover in this world is both a unity and plurality. Each number can be both a unity and a plurality by being harmoniously put together; for harmony is a plurality made into a unity.

The opposites that are harmoniously united to form number are the odd and the even. These are inseparably woven into harmony with each other by a wonderful and divine Nature. From this harmony of the odd and the even come principles and methods that show us that what is beautiful and limited and subject to knowledge is prior to the ugly, unlimited, and incomprehensible. The parts of the unlimited are given shape and boundaries by numbers, and like everything measured, the unlimited takes on a likeness to what measures it.

From this study of numbers, the rational part of the soul, which is limited and definite, will put in order the irrational parts, that is, the emotions and desires, which are unlimited and confused. These latter are like forms of inequality and are ruled and measured by the rational part through equality. From this equalizing process, we gain gentleness, courage, endurance, and the ability to take control of ourselves. The study of arithmetic is therefore the best preparation for the study of philosophy and for the practice of a virtuous life.

The Value of Science
by Henri Poincaré

The search for truth should be the goal of our activities. No other goal is worthy of us. Shouldn't one first make the effort to decrease human misery? No! That is a negative goal and could be better achieved by the destruction of the world. If we wish increasingly to free man from material burdens, hunger, and poverty, it is so that he can be free to study and contemplate truth.

But truth can sometimes frighten us. It is sometimes deceptive. It is a phantom that shows itself for a moment only to flee endlessly from our grasp. And truth is also cruel. We often wonder if illusion isn't more consoling, for it gives us confidence. If illusion vanishes, will hope remain, and will we still have the courage to act? The horse harnessed to the treadmill would refuse to budge if his eyes were not covered. To seek truth we must be independent.

First by truth I mean scientific truth, but I also mean to include moral truth. It may seem that I misuse words by calling both of these truth. They have nothing in common. Scientific truth is demonstrated, moral truth is felt. But I can't separate them; anyone who loves one loves the other. To find either, the soul must be completely free of prejudice and emotions. Our souls must attain absolute sincerity. We shouldn't fear moral truth, and we shouldn't dread scientific truth. First of all, they can't conflict. Science and morality have their own domains, which touch but don't overlap. Morality shows us the goals we should have, science teaches us how to attain them. They never conflict since they never meet. There cannot be immoral science, any more than there can be scientific morals.

When we fear science, it is primarily because it cannot give us happiness. We are attracted by the image of the contented animal that seems to suffer less than man. But can we really long for the early paradise where man was immortal because he didn't know he would die? Once we have tasted the apple, no suffering ever makes us forget its flavor. We always return to it. We cannot be happy through science, but today we would be less happy without it.

With what tool then can we reach scientific truth when we recognize just how different and variable scientific intelligence is? A geometer's mind is very different from a physicist's or a naturalist's. Even mathematicians' minds do not resemble one another's. Some mathematicians only recognize logic, others only use intuition and imagination. Shouldn't this make us distrust the possibility that minds so different reach and use the same mathematical truths? Can a truth that is not the same for all be truth? But when we look more closely, we see that the logical and the intuitive join in the common mathematical talk that neither could achieve alone.

The next concern about reaching scientific truth concerns the mathematical language that the mathematicians present to the scientists. It is useful, but shouldn't one worry that these artificial symbols may be like a veil placed between the eye of the physicist and reality? No, far from it! Without these artificially constructed mathematical languages, the most intimate resemblances and analogies between things would have remained unknown to us.

We would have remained ignorant of the internal harmony of the world, which is, in fact, the only true objective reality.

The best expression of this internal harmony of the world is scientific law. Scientific law is one of the most recent achievements of the human mind. There are, indeed, people who live as if there were countless miracles and aren't astonished by them. But we should be astonished by nature's regularity. Some men demand that their gods prove their existence by miracles. But, the eternal marvel is that all miracles have causes. The world is divine because it is a harmony of laws. If we always found miracles, how would we ever know that this showed us gods and not a world ruled by chance?

The advance of science is not like the changes in a city where old buildings are pitilessly torn down and replaced by new ones. Rather, it is like the continuous evolution of an organic being. Animals evolve endlessly and finally are not recognizable any longer. But the expert eye still finds traces of the prior work and the changes. So one must not think that old fashioned scientific theories either were or have become sterile and useless.

Finally, one must ask whether the harmony which human intelligence thinks it discovers in nature really exists outside of our own intelligence. No doubt a reality that is entirely independent of the mind that thinks it, or sees or feels it, is an impossibility. A world as exterior as that would be forever inaccessible to us. But what we call objective or scientific reality is what is common to many thinking beings and could be common to all of us. This common part can only be the harmony expressed by mathematical laws. This harmony in mathematical laws is the only objective or true reality. When we recognize that the universal harmony of the world is the source of all beauty, we will understand what value we should attach to the slow and painful progress that, little by little, enables us to know it better.

Discussion Evaluation Form

The items below are discussion dynamics that may or may not be present in your group. Decide to what extent you think that each dynamic was present in the discussion. Then decide whether you think the group needs to work to improve in this area.

	None Some Great deal	Need to Improve?
Dominance by some individuals	1 2 3 4 5 6 7 8 9 10	Yes ❏ No ❏
Cooperation	1 2 3 4 5 6 7 8 9 10	Yes ❏ No ❏
Silence	1 2 3 4 5 6 7 8 9 10	Yes ❏ No ❏
Interrupting	1 2 3 4 5 6 7 8 9 10	Yes ❏ No ❏
Respect	1 2 3 4 5 6 7 8 9 10	Yes ❏ No ❏
Balanced participation	1 2 3 4 5 6 7 8 9 10	Yes ❏ No ❏
Active listening	1 2 3 4 5 6 7 8 9 10	Yes ❏ No ❏
Lack of interest	1 2 3 4 5 6 7 8 9 10	Yes ❏ No ❏
Asking one other questions	1 2 3 4 5 6 7 8 9 10	Yes ❏ No ❏
Building on one other's contributions	1 2 3 4 5 6 7 8 9 10	Yes ❏ No ❏
Many people talking at once	1 2 3 4 5 6 7 8 9 10	Yes ❏ No ❏

Pick one of the dynamics that you think the group should work to improve, and explain why.

How would you rate this discussion on a scale of 1–10? _____

Illegitimate Power

Our earliest historical records show us that not all rulers were legitimate. Often power was seized in a way that constituted an abuse of the tradition of a particular society. The succession of Egyptian dynasties, for example, indicates various struggles for control that went on for thousands of years. In Greece, the title of tyrant was not, as it is with us, the name for a tyrannical ruler but for one who had seized the power over the city-state by means that were not sanctioned. The struggle between Saul and David over who was anointed by God suggests how complex the question of who is the rightful ruler can become. Shakespeare's plays, the First and Second Parts of King Henry IV, attempt to explore how a new form of legitimate kingship and therefore power can arise after a legitimate king—Richard II—is overthrown and murdered. In the eighteenth century, many thinkers in France and the American colonies expanded the ideas about the foundations of government and the nature of the sovereign. In particular, they asked what would be required to establish a ruling power that was legitimate. Jean Jacques Rousseau and Jefferson agreed that what was required was the consent of the governed.

Our more recent awareness of illegitimate power is not focused on usurpations or lack of representation or palace revolutions. Instead, the instances of the exercise of illegitimate power many people find most vivid in recent history are slavery and the Holocaust. Through this unit's texts and worksheet, we will consider slavery and genocide, two variants of enslaving others through the illegitimate use of power that were both at one time legal.

The situations of the Holocaust and slavery raise some similar issues. In both circumstances, the perpetrators considered the victims to be of a different species. The Jews and African Americans were viewed as objects rather than as persons.

There are also significant differences. Historically, one justification made for slavery contends that certain beings are better off as slaves because they cannot take care of themselves in the world. Thus, this justification goes, it is the role of the master to rule the slave for his or her own good. Aristotle presented the classic example of such a justification.

He claimed that certain people are slaves by nature. He argued that some people cannot reason for themselves but can follow the direction of others who can use their reason. Such people are the natural slaves, and it is to their benefit to be ruled. Aristotle was in fact taking a progressive step in his time by distinguishing between those who were enslaved by conquest and who were not necessarily natural slaves and those who were slaves by nature. Aristotle was probably thinking of people we consider as having various mental disabilities. Furthermore, his approach places great responsibility on the master to care for those in his or her power. However, Aristotle's argument was used in Europe and in the United States to justify even the most horrifying forms of slavery. The Nazis' justification for enslaving and exterminating Jews, Gypsies, and people from many other ethnic groups was somewhat different. They contended that many groups of people were inferior and could and should be enslaved and ultimately exterminated in order to further the development of a specific elite race. These inferior peoples included Slavs, Jews, Africans, and Gypsies.

The texts for this unit consider the perspective and frame of mind of the perpetrators of such crimes. What does it mean to enslave another person or to commit genocide? The readings suggest that a person can act either intentionally or thoughtlessly in exercising power unjustly. Olaudah Equiano sees the slave owner's action as intentional; Hannah Arendt considers the action of a particular Nazi leader, Eichmann, to have been in an odd way thoughtless, almost mechanical. We must ask how one could be thoughtful about enslaving others. And also, we must ask how one could be thoughtless about such a task as exterminating a people. As we consider these things, we can also think about examples of both the considered and the thoughtless abuse of power as we have seen it arise in the discussion process itself. What do the dynamics of our own group reveal to us about the exercise of power in human relations?

As we form a discussion group, the traditional role of the leader or teacher or professor is modified. In our day-to-day experience, the location of power is built into many of our activities. This presence of power gives the person or persons holding it an essential and therefore legitimate role to play. A president or governor signing bills into law or making political appointments, a policeman directing traffic, or a referee at an athletic event are instances of someone possessing and exercising legitimate power. In the army, there is a hierarchy of ranks, each of which has a specific role and therefore the power to accomplish certain tasks. These are roles that possess power because of the structure of our society. There are also more conditional situations. There are people with specific forms of expertise. When that knowledge is required, we all defer to the authority of the person or profession and bestow power for longer or shorter periods of time. However, a discussion differs from either of these situations. It changes our expected roles and its evolution invites us to rethink our attitudes about power and its use and abuse.

An example may make this clearer. In a recent discussion class, a group of first-year college students was engaged in a highly cooperative and sustained exploration of a text and a topic. The leader was delighted that he could hold back and watch the discussion evolve. Suddenly, a student spoke up and entirely changed the direction of the conversation. Startled, the leader and others moved it back to the question the group had been pursuing. Afterward, the student somewhat indignantly approached the discussion leader. The student wanted to know why the leader had acted that way since the leader had told the class at the start of the term that the group had to share responsibility for the direction and success of the discussions. The student believed that he was doing just that. The student had wanted to change the direction of the exploration and had taken the initiative to do so. This is an interesting case of power misused. The student acted without any thought of the needs and progress of the rest of the group. The student wanted something to happen and, somewhat unknowingly, treated the other members of the group as objects. He thought he was being helpful.

Several examples of abuse can occur within a discussion. For instance, a participant can refer to a passage in the text in a seemingly helpful way. However, sometimes in a discussion, a participant is actually using a textual reference as a device to assert power over the discussion. Another instance occurs when we entirely neglect to respond to what someone has just said. We speak as if that person had not spoken, as if the other participant were making noise that we simply ignore. These are brief episodes that can happen either intentionally or unthinkingly and that may seem insignificant. However, they contain the seeds of the deeper issues explored in the texts.

Worksheet 4

The texts by Equiano and Arendt take up horrifying examples of the illegitimate use of power and its effects both on those over whom it is exercised and on those who employ it. The unit's introduction suggests that the problem of illegitimate power is also one we must consider in situations closer to home, even in our everyday interactions with one another. In the worksheet, we consider roles in which power is held legitimately and ask how likely it is in each that the legitimate use of power might verge into an abuse of power.

1. The following people hold power over others either generally or in certain situations. How would you rank them with regard to how likely it is that they would abuse their power? Rank each position on a scale of 1 to 10, with 1 being the least likely to abuse power and 10 being the most likely.

   _____ a) Doctor

   _____ b) Federal prosecutor

   _____ c) Military official

   _____ d) Prison guard

   _____ e) Teacher

   _____ f) Police officer

   _____ g) Psychiatrist

   _____ h) State governor

   _____ i) Biological parent

   _____ j) Stepparent

2. Choose an item that you ranked with a 1 (or the item to which you gave your lowest ranking) and an item that you ranked with a 10 (or the item to which you gave your highest ranking). Briefly explain your ranking of these items.

3. After reading the texts, write an opening question.

The Interesting Narrative of the Life of Olaudah Equiano, or Gustavus Vassa, the African

by Olaudah Equiano

These practices were not confined to particular places or individuals. In all the different islands in which I have been (and I have visited no less than 15), the treatment of slaves has been nearly the same. Indeed, the history of slavery in one island or even on one plantation might well serve as a history for the whole practice. The slave trade destroys men's minds and hardens them to every feeling of humanity. For I refuse to believe that the dealers in slaves are born worse than other men. No, it is the result of this mistaken greed that it corrupts the milk of human kindness and turns it into bitter gall. Had these men pursued different activities, they might have been as generous, as tenderhearted, and as just as they are now unfeeling, greedy, and cruel. Surely, this trade in slaves cannot be good. It spreads like a disease and changes everything it touches. It violates the first natural rights of mankind—equality and independence.

The practice of slavery gives one man a rule and a dominion over his fellow men that God could never have intended. It raises the slave owner to a state far above a human being, for it forces the slave into a position below it. One pretends to be a god, the other is made an animal. Through the arrogance of human pride, it places a difference between them that is immeasurable in distance and endless in time. Yet how mistaken and self-defeating is even the owner's greed! Are slaves more useful by being made animals than they would be if they were allowed to be men? When you make men slaves, you take away half of their virtue and ability. And by your own action you set for them the example of fraud, rape, and cruelty. You force them to live in a state of war with you, and then you complain that they are not honest or faithful. You beat them, you keep them ignorant, and then you claim that they cannot learn. You claim their minds are such poor soil that education would be lost on them. Yet they come originally from a climate where nature has given great riches to everything. Should we think that men from there alone were left unfinished and incapable of enjoying the treasures nature has poured out for them? Such a claim is absurd!

Why do you use those instruments of torture? Should one rational being use them on another? Aren't you ashamed to see people of the same nature as you brought so low? And aren't there great dangers for you in treating others this way? Aren't you always afraid of revolt by them? But by changing your conduct and treating your slaves as men, every cause of fear would be banished. They would be faithful, intelligent, and vigorous; and peace, prosperity, and happiness would be yours.

Banality and Conscience
by Hannah Arendt

There is of course no doubt that the defendant and the nature of his acts as well as the trial itself raise problems of a general nature that go far beyond the matters considered in Jerusalem. I have attempted to go into some of these problems in the Epilogue, which ceases to be simple reporting. I would not have been surprised if people had found my treatment inadequate, and I would have welcomed a discussion of the general significance of the entire body of facts, which could have been all the more meaningful the more directly it referred to the concrete events. I also can well imagine that an authentic controversy might have arisen over the subtitle of the book; for when I speak of the banality of evil, I do so only on the strictly factual level, pointing to a phenomenon that stared one in the face at the trial. Eichmann was not Iago and not Macbeth, and nothing would have been farther from his mind than to determine with Richard III "to prove a villain." Except for an extraordinary diligence in looking out for his personal advancement, he had no motives at all. And this diligence in itself was in no way criminal; he certainly would never have murdered his superior in order to inherit his post. He merely, to put the matter colloquially, never realized what he was doing. It was precisely this lack of imagination which enabled him to sit for months on end facing a German Jew who was conducting the police interrogation, pouring out this heart to the man and explaining again and again how it was that he reached the rank of lieutenant colonel in the S.S. and that it had not been his fault that he was not promoted. In principle he knew quite well what it was all about, and in his final statement to the court he spoke of the "revaluation of values prescribed by the [Nazi] government." He was not stupid. It was sheer thoughtlessness—something by no means identical with stupidity—that predisposed him to become one of the greatest criminals of that period. And if this is "banal" and even funny—if with the best will in the world one cannot extract any diabolical or demonic profundity from Eichmann—that is still far from calling it commonplace. It surely cannot be so common that a man facing death, and, moreover, standing beneath the gallows, should be able to think of nothing but what he has heard at funerals all his life, and these "lofty words" should completely becloud the reality of his own death. That such remoteness from reality and such thoughtlessness can wreak more havoc than all the evil instincts taken together that, perhaps, are inherent in man—that was, in fact, the lesson one could learn in Jerusalem. But it was a lesson, neither an explanation of the phenomenon nor a theory about it.

Seemingly more complicated, but in reality far simpler than examining the strange interdependence of thoughtlessness and evil, is the question of what kind of crime is actually involved here; a crime, moreover, which all agree is unprecedented. For the concept of genocide, introduced explicitly to cover a crime unknown before, although applicable up to a point is not fully adequate, for the simple reason that massacres of whole peoples are not unprecedented. They were the order of the day in antiquity, and the centuries of colonization and imperialism; the English deliberately rejected such procedures as a means of maintaining their rule over India. The phrase has the virtue of dispelling the prejudice that such monstrous acts can be committed only against a foreign nation or a different race. There is the well-known fact that Hitler began his mass murders by granting "mercy deaths" to the "incurably ill," and that he intended to wind up his extermination program by doing away with "genetically damaged" Germans (heart and lung patients). But quite aside from that, it is apparent that this sort of killing can be directed against any given group, that is, that the principle of selection is dependent only upon circumstantial factors. It is quite conceivable that in the automated economy of a not-too-distant future, men may be tempted to exterminate all those whose intelligence quotient is below a certain level.

Of course it is important to the political and social sciences that the essence of totalitarian government, and perhaps the nature of every bureaucracy, is to make functionaries and mere cogs in the administrative machinery out of men, and thus to dehumanize them. And one can debate long and profitably on the rule of Nobody, which is what the political form known as bureaucracy truly is. Only one must realize clearly that the administration of justice can consider these factors only to the extent that they are circumstances of the crime; just as, in a case of theft, the economic plight of the thief is taken into account without excusing the theft, let alone wiping it off the slate. True, we have become very much accustomed by modern psychology and sociology, not to speak of modern bureaucracy, to explaining away the responsibility of the doer for his deed in terms of this or that kind of determinism. Whether such seemingly deeper explanations of human actions are right or wrong is debatable. But what is not debatable is that no judicial procedure would be possible on the basis of them, and that the administration of justice, measured by such theories, is an extremely un-modern, not to say outmoded, institution. When Hitler said that a day would come in Germany when it would be considered a "disgrace" to be a jurist, he was speaking with utter consistency of his dream of a perfect bureaucracy.

Discussion Evaluation Form

The items below are discussion dynamics that may or may not be present in your group. Decide to what extent you think that each dynamic was present in the discussion. Then decide whether you think the group needs to work to improve in this area.

	None Some Great deal	Need to Improve?
Dominance by some individuals	1 2 3 4 5 6 7 8 9 10	Yes ❏ No ❏
Cooperation	1 2 3 4 5 6 7 8 9 10	Yes ❏ No ❏
Silence	1 2 3 4 5 6 7 8 9 10	Yes ❏ No ❏
Interrupting	1 2 3 4 5 6 7 8 9 10	Yes ❏ No ❏
Respect	1 2 3 4 5 6 7 8 9 10	Yes ❏ No ❏
Balanced participation	1 2 3 4 5 6 7 8 9 10	Yes ❏ No ❏
Active listening	1 2 3 4 5 6 7 8 9 10	Yes ❏ No ❏
Lack of interest	1 2 3 4 5 6 7 8 9 10	Yes ❏ No ❏
Asking one other questions	1 2 3 4 5 6 7 8 9 10	Yes ❏ No ❏
Building on one other's contributions	1 2 3 4 5 6 7 8 9 10	Yes ❏ No ❏
Many people talking at once	1 2 3 4 5 6 7 8 9 10	Yes ❏ No ❏

Pick one of the dynamics that you think the group should work to improve, and explain why.

How would you rate this discussion on a scale of 1–10? _____

5

Group History and Ownership

The development of a discussion group takes time. The process of exploring and modifying our habits is gradual. These habits are not merely personal characteristics but also part of our cultural inheritance—part of our group's history. They have evolved over hundreds and even thousands of years and are part of the fabric of our culture. They are also what enable us to work within our society's institutions. However, we must evaluate these habits consciously to determine which ones are still appropriate and which ones are counterproductive remnants of once-useful skills. Every group will face the issues of the locus of power, the tension between competition and cooperation, and the difficulty in remaining open to new ideas. We will also have to make the effort to surrender ownership of the things we think we know best—such as topics that we have spent time studying or experiences that we have had—and allow others to comment on them. In addition to the difficulties we face as individuals, however, each group has a unique history and shared struggle as it progresses to a point at which each member takes ownership of the discussion. The ways in which groups change over time depend on many factors, including the individuals who are members of the group and their personal relations and willingness to examine their own presuppositions. The factors influencing change affect all groups, regardless of their country of origin or their background.

Because our educational system and the hierarchies in our society's institutions all place a remarkably high premium on the possession and communication of expertise, each of our Touchstones sessions will uncover certain successes and problems as we strive to change our attitudes toward expertise. We will have to work to overcome the habits and expectations we have developed about who has a right to speak and contribute. The specific forms that these problems and successes take will be in part a function of the participants' backgrounds and situations. For instance, the members of a discussion group of investment bankers were very expert initially at asking one another questions; they were highly skilled at eliciting information from others. However, because they were accustomed to working in a highly competitive environment, they all tended to attempt to dominate one another. This of course made it difficult for them to build on one another's contributions. Groups of prisoners often find it difficult to focus on the text but, because any sign of disrespect in a prison environment is a great risk to one's safety, the inmates generally become successful at listening and responding to one another.

In addition to the professional or institutional background of the group, the individual participants' strengths and weaknesses also help determine how a particular group will succeed and develop in the course of its evolution. In any group, there are people of many different types, and a discussion environment brings out fascinating and often unexpected characteristics. Some people love to offer their opinions and don't mind at all if others attack them or make them recant. Others will only offer ideas once they trust the rest of the group members to make the effort to understand them. Some people like playing devil's advocate and will present positions just to try those positions out. Others feel very vulnerable about the open-ended nature of the discussions. Some people love to make intuitive leaps but need help from others to detail the reasons. Others are very analytic but less imaginative about possible lines of interpretation. Each person has a unique perspective and collection of talents and experience. It will be our joint task as the group evolves to recognize and draw on the strengths of all the participants.

One of our greatest resources in accomplishing this task is the texts. In a Touchstones Discussion, the texts not only present us with material to consider, they also function as tools. As we consider our goals for our discussion group, both for the next meeting as well as the long-term future, we should ask how the discussion of these particular texts might move us in the desired direction or assist us in overcoming problems that we have encountered. For example, on one hand, a text on a highly controversial or emotionally charged topic may encourage a high level of active participation from many members of the group; however, we should also be aware that such a topic may make listening difficult. On the other hand, a difficult and abstract text may offer a safe place for shyer, more studious members of the group to enter the process and offer their strengths to the group; however, other participants may find such a text alienating. Every text presents us with a variety of opportunities and potential difficulties that we must evaluate carefully as we consider what approach might be most helpful at a particular point in the evolution of our group.

Look over your discussion evaluation sheet from the last session and select one of the areas you marked as a problem. As you read the texts for this meeting, decide how these texts might be used to overcome the particular difficulty you judged that your group encountered. Both texts—Saint Augustine's Confessions and R. G. Collingwood's An Autobiography—are authors' accounts of their youths and particularly of their attitudes toward study and learning at that stage of their lives. Would you expect this sort of autobiographical account to encourage a high level of participation in your group discussion? Might it lead the participants to share personal narratives of their own? Is the topic of study, and the way in which it is approached, likely to lead to heated exchanges or an orderly discussion? Perhaps the previous discussion had many silences. If so, you should ask yourself whether this unit's texts are ones about which many in the group will have opinions and whether they would be willing to state these publicly.

The worksheet for this unit asks you questions about these considerations, and about how you might use the text as a tool to assist the development of the discussion group. Early on in the meeting, you will gather in small groups to compare your judgments on these issues.

Worksheet 5

The introduction highlights the fact that each discussion group is unique in having its own history, its own institutional context, and its own particular mix of participants. The text becomes a tool—our ally—as we attempt to help our group members discover our strengths and work together most effectively. This unit's readings by Saint Augustine of Hippo and R. G. Collingwood are both autobiographical. Thus they each raise the question of how our histories help make us who we are. The worksheet asks us to think about how these particular texts and the set of questions they raise might become a useful tool for us, given our own group history and situation.

1. Which problem from the last session did you choose to work to improve on?

2. How could this unit's texts help you to solve that problem?

3. After your second reading of the texts, consider the following positive qualities in a discussion. Rate how well this unit's paired texts can help you achieve each quality. Use a scale of 1 to 10, with 1 being not very effectively and 10 being very effectively. For example, if you think that these texts will encourage the group to focus on the given quality, you might assign that quality an 8 or a 9. If you think that it is unlikely that these texts will foster the development of say, cooperation, you might rate the quality of cooperation as a 2 or a 3.

   _____ Cooperation   _____ Balanced participation

   _____ Building on one other's contributions   _____ Respectful participation

   _____ Participants assisting one another   _____ Active listening

   _____ Asking one another questions   _____ Responding to one another

   _____ Other_____

4. For your lowest ranking, please give a brief reason for your decision.

5. For your highest ranking, please give a brief reason for your decision.

6. What opening question on these texts might help solve the group dynamics problem you chose to work on from the last session?

The Confessions
by Saint Augustine of Hippo

As a boy, I did not care for lessons and I disliked being forced to study. All the same, I was compelled to learn, and good came to me as a result, although it was not of my own doing. For I would not have studied at all if I had not been made to do so, and what a person does against his will is not to his own credit.

Even now, I cannot fully understand why I so much disliked the study of the Greek language, though I loved my own language, Latin. In both cases, the early lessons were tiresome, but far more valuable than those that followed. For those early lessons gave me the power which I still have, of reading whatever is set before me, and writing whatever I wish to write. The later lessons in Latin told of adventures and love. But why did I dislike Greek literature, even including Homer? Homer, as well as Virgil, was a teller of tales. I think I learned Latin because I wanted to learn it, without fear or being forced by threats of punishments. With Greek, I was constantly subjected to violent threats and cruel punishment to make me learn. This clearly shows that we learn better in a free spirit of curiosity than under fear and compulsion.

Let me tell you, my God, how I wasted the brains you gave me on foolish daydreams. I was set a task which bothered me, and for which, if I were successful, I would win praise; if not, I was afraid of disgrace and a beating. I had to recite the speech of Juno, who was angry and hurt because she could not prevent Aeneas from sailing to Italy. The contest was to be won by the boy who found the best words to suit the meaning and best expressed the feeling of sorrow and anger of someone as great as Juno.

A student causes more offense if he breaks the laws of grammar and pronunciation and says "human beings" without the "h" than if, being a human being himself, he were to break your laws and hate other human beings. Certainly, no kind of learning comes as close as this sort of competition to the judgment against conscience, that is, "You do to someone else what you would not like done to you." A student, trying to win a reputation as being clever, will attack his fellow students with fury and hatred. He will take great care that he does not mispronounce the word "human." But he will be indifferent whether his rage and fury have the effect of utterly shaming and destroying another human being.

What did all this matter to me, my God? Why did my recitation win more praise than the recitations of all the other boys in my class? What shameful pride! Was there no other subject I could have sharpened my mind and my tongue on? I might have used them, O Lord, to praise you in the words in Scripture. But instead, by doing as I was told, I won praise from the people whose favor I sought, for I thought that the right way to live was to do as they wished. In your eyes, O Lord, nothing could be more shameful than I was then, since I was even a trouble to the people whom I set out to please. Many a time I lied to my teacher and my parents and deceived them, because I wanted to play games or watch some worthless show. I even stole from my parents' cupboards, either from greed or to get something to exchange with other boys. And I often cheated at the games I played with other boys simply because the vain desire to win got the better of me. Yet, I became furious if I found others cheating on me.

Can this be simply because I was a child? No, O Lord! For as we get older and older, these same passions remain with us, just as more severe punishments follow upon those we experienced in school.

An Autobiography
by R. G. Collingwood

My father had plenty of books and allowed me to read them as I pleased. Among others, he had kept the books of classical scholarship, ancient history, and philosophy that he had used at Oxford University. Usually, I left these books alone. But one day when I was eight years old, curiosity made me take down a little black book with the title *Kant's Theory of Ethics*. As I began reading it, my small body wedged between the bookcase and the table, I was attacked by a strange series of emotions.

First came an intense excitement. I felt that things of the highest importance were being said about matters that, at all costs, I must understand. Then, with a wave of frustration, came the discovery that I could not understand them. I was ashamed to have to confess that here was a book whose words were English, and whose sentences were grammatical, but whose meaning escaped me. Then, third and last, came the strangest emotion of all. I felt that the contents of this book, although I could not understand it, were somehow my business. The contents of this book were a matter personal to myself, or rather to some future self of my own. It was not like the common childish intention to "be a truck driver when I grow up," for there was not desire in this emotion. I did not, in any ordinary sense of the word, "want" to understand Kant's *Ethics* when I should be old enough. But I felt as if a veil had been lifted and my destiny revealed.

There came upon me by degrees, after this, a sense of being burdened with a task whose nature I could not define except by saying, "I must think." What I was to think about I did not know. When I became silent or absent minded in company, or tried to be alone in order to think without interruption, I could not have said, and still cannot say, what it was that I actually thought. There were no particular questions that I asked myself. There were not special objects upon which I directed my mind. There was only a shapeless and aimless intellectual disturbance, as if I were wrestling with a fog.

I know now that this is what always happens when I am in the early stages of work on a problem. Until the problem is almost solved, I do not know what it is. All I am conscious of is a vague disturbance in my mind, a sense of being worried about I cannot say what. I know now that the problems that would occupy me all my life were taking their first shape deep down inside me. But anyone who observed me must have thought, as my elders did, that I had fallen into the habit of loafing. It seemed to them that I had lost the alertness and quickness of mind so noticeable in my early childhood. My only defense against this opinion, since I did not know and therefore could not explain what was happening to me, was to cover up these moods with some trivial and automatic physical activity. I was good with my hands, and liked to walk, bicycle, row, and sail. So when this mood came upon me, I would make something quite uninteresting, like a regiment of paper soldiers, or wander aimlessly in the woods, or sail all day in a dead calm. It was painful to be laughed at for playing with paper soldiers, but to explain why I did it was impossible.

Whether it was this growing idleness that made my father send me to school, I am not sure. I felt it a matter of honor to try to win scholarships. I did this, if for no other reason, than to justify the spending on me of all that money. However, even if I had not specialized my interests in order to know enough to win prizes, the English system of education would have forced me to do it. This I consider the greatest evil of English schools. It haunts our classrooms, the ghost of a silly argument over 300 years old. Teachers and students are infected with the lunatic idea that studies must be either "classical" or "modern" and that every student must specialize in one or the other. I was equally well fitted to specialize in Greek or Latin, or in modern history and languages, or in the natural sciences. And nothing could have nourished my mind more than to study all three. But I was forced to specialize in one of them, and since my father's teaching had given me a good deal more Latin and Greek than other boys of my age possessed, I specialized in that and became a "classical scholar."

Discussion Evaluation Form

The items below are discussion dynamics that may or may not be present in your group. Decide to what extent you think that each dynamic was present in the discussion. Then decide whether you think the group needs to work to improve in this area.

	None Some Great deal	Need to Improve?
Dominance by some individuals	1 2 3 4 5 6 7 8 9 10	Yes ❏ No ❏
Cooperation	1 2 3 4 5 6 7 8 9 10	Yes ❏ No ❏
Silence	1 2 3 4 5 6 7 8 9 10	Yes ❏ No ❏
Interrupting	1 2 3 4 5 6 7 8 9 10	Yes ❏ No ❏
Respect	1 2 3 4 5 6 7 8 9 10	Yes ❏ No ❏
Balanced participation	1 2 3 4 5 6 7 8 9 10	Yes ❏ No ❏
Active listening	1 2 3 4 5 6 7 8 9 10	Yes ❏ No ❏
Lack of interest	1 2 3 4 5 6 7 8 9 10	Yes ❏ No ❏
Asking one other questions	1 2 3 4 5 6 7 8 9 10	Yes ❏ No ❏
Building on one other's contributions	1 2 3 4 5 6 7 8 9 10	Yes ❏ No ❏
Many people talking at once	1 2 3 4 5 6 7 8 9 10	Yes ❏ No ❏

Pick one of the dynamics that you think the group should work to improve, and explain why.

How would you rate this discussion on a scale of 1–10? ____

Participant Questionnaire

In the best discussions, each person acts simultaneously as a participant and a leader. Furthermore, each group member acts with the interests of the group in mind and governs his or her participation accordingly. This self-evaluation form helps you reflect on your participation and recognize areas in which you would like to improve.

How much would you say that you participate?

❑ Less than most ❑ About average ❑ More than most

How often do you interrupt others?

❑ Very Little ❑ Sometimes ❑ Often ❑ All the time

How often do you listen to all the participants?

❑ Very Little ❑ Sometimes ❑ Often ❑ All the time

How often do you solicit other opinions?

❑ Very Little ❑ Sometimes ❑ Often ❑ All the time

How often do you build on what others say?

❑ Very Little ❑ Sometimes ❑ Often ❑ All the time

How often do you keep focused and on task?

❑ Very Little ❑ Sometimes ❑ Often ❑ All the time

How often do you encourage quieter participants to speak?

❑ Very Little ❑ Sometimes ❑ Often ❑ All the time

How often do you prepare well for the sessions?

❑ Very Little ❑ Sometimes ❑ Often ❑ All the time

What is one way in which you have improved as a participant?

Name one way that you would like to improve as a participant.

Stage 2

Legitimate Speakers

6

The Difference between
Our Public and Private Selves

Almost all of us have grown up in a culture that is dominated by Western ideas, by science and technology, and by the corporations and institutions within which we work and learn. Each of us therefore shares a certain range of concepts and presuppositions—what is often called a paradigm—within which we make our choices and live our lives. We certainly could not function without the frameworks that our presuppositions and assumptions provide. Yet our inability to recognize these characteristic patterns of thought and to notice how such patterns shape our lives often keeps us from understanding other perspectives and from exploring all the possibilities within a given situation. Our tendency to regard the lens through which we habitually view our world as the only possible or legitimate perspective is often the strongest impediment to implementing real change in our lives on either a personal or an institutional level.

Although each of us comes equipped with certain presuppositions as part of our common cultural heritage, each of us differs in the emphases he or she places on these shared attitudes. It is similar to the way in which we all share a common language yet display different styles of speaking and writing. Through taking a closer look at these differences, we should be able to see more clearly both the ways in which each of us is unique and the ways in which common beliefs and habits of mind shape us all.

One of the most basic distinctions we make in our lives is the one between our public or professional and our private lives. We all have certain attitudes that determine how we behave in activities that occur in the public realm and other, frequently quite different, attitudes that influence our behavior among those closest to us—family and friends. This division, however, is not universal. There at least seem to be societies in which people's lives occur almost entirely in what we would consider the public realm. This public living appears to be the case in many Native American societies and was also the case in the ancient Greek city of Sparta. In China, although there is a distinction between the society at large and the family, the family seems to be subordinated virtually completely to social responsibilities. In our society, however, people entirely absorbed in the public realm are often considered workaholics and told to get a life. Of course there is no society in which people are entirely absorbed in the private realm; that would be a sort of contradiction. The closest description we have of that situation is Homer's picture in the *Odyssey* of the Cyclopes who live in caves alone or with their families with each, as Homer says, being a law unto himself. How to adjust our public and private selves is one of the great tasks we all face. How our professional lives and personal lives can fit harmoniously together is one of the great issues facing our society as new forms of family and institutional life emerge.

Another distinction that underlies our thinking is the contrast we make between objective facts and subjective feelings. Most people believe that objectivity is an important quality in determining what is correct, fair, or true about the world. We worry about how our judgments are colored by our attitudes and biases. When we are told that we are not being objective, we generally feel the need to defend ourselves. And although none of us achieves complete objectivity, we think it is an ideal. The tremendous success of science in the last 300 years has made objectivity a model for other forms of activity.

Yet although we all believe to a large extent in the virtues of objectivity, we also probably think that this attitude can be pushed too far. We tend to be shocked when we hear of objectivity becoming an overriding consideration in our private or family lives. For instance, we resist the idea that friends are simply people who can be useful to us in certain quantifiable ways. People from Western nations are also frequently troubled when they hear about arranged marriages in other parts of the world. An arranged marriage appears to violate deep beliefs about human feeling and emotion and about choice and freedom. However, arranged marriages have worked for thousands of years, and entire societies that have achieved great historical prominence have been based on them. Even in our society, objective concerns do play some part in selecting a marriage partner. When we hear about couples in which each partner is very different in education, background, and aspirations, we wonder whether the union will last even while we hope that love will conquer all. Similar issues arise in business and corporate environments. Objectivity is, on the one hand, admired, but on the other hand, often viewed as a dehumanizing attitude that looks only to the bottom line. We tend to criticize the heartless technocrat along with the arranger of marriages. What is the proper relationship between these various attitudes, between subjectivity and objectivity, between our public and private lives?

The two texts bear precisely on this issue. They describe the same sort of event but from two very different perspectives. Thucydides and Albert Camus both write about the plague—Thucydides writes of the outbreak in Athens in the second year of the Peloponnesian War between Athens and Sparta; Camus writes of a fictional outbreak in northern Africa. One account is a dispassionate objective narration, the other is a description of a doctor who is struggling to recognize and imagine the reality of the disease. Through these two texts that focus on the same type of event as well as the worksheet, we can examine the objective and subjective and the public and personal.

Worksheet 6

The unit's introduction highlighted the ways in which we separate our lives into the public and private realms and the differences in our behavior and assumptions within these divisions. The worksheet asks us to consider these differences for a number of specific cases. In the texts by Thucydides and Camus, we have examples of extreme situations in which the divisions and structures we use to order our lives are broken down and also examples of the drive we have to find normalcy by reclaiming our roles and the "proper" division between the public and private realms.

1. For each contrasting pair of beliefs or attitudes on the next page, think about how great a role each should play in the public and private dimensions of our lives. Then, express your view by dividing 10 points between the items of each pair. For example, suppose we view the pair of objectivity and subjectivity in relation to our public lives. One might think that objectivity should heavily outweigh subjectivity but both should be present. On that basis, one might allocate 9 to objectivity and 1 to subjectivity. Or, one might agree that both should be present but believe that they should be more balanced and allocate the points as 6 and 4, respectively. For our private or personal lives, you would then also decide how to allocate 10 points. Here, for example, one might think subjectivity is most important, but also assign objectivity 3 points because subjective approaches should still rely somewhat on facts.

	Public Realm	Private Realm
a) Objectivity	_____	_____
Subjectivity	_____ 10	_____ 10
b) Efficiency	_____	_____
Spontaneity	_____ 10	_____ 10
c) Skeptical attitude toward others	_____	_____
Trusting attitude toward others	_____ 10	_____ 10
d) Problems have a definite, unambiguous solution	_____	_____
Problems solved by compromise between the parties	_____ 10	_____ 10
e) Risk taking	_____	_____
Risk minimizing	_____ 10	_____ 10

2. After reading the texts, write an opening question for the discussion.

The Peloponnesian War
by Thucydides

Soon after the Spartans invaded the area around Athens, the plague first appeared among the Athenians. No one could remember an epidemic of such magnitude and seriousness, and the doctors themselves were not, at first, of any use. They didn't know how to treat it, and as they spent the most time with the ill, the doctors were the first to die. And no other human art did any better. Prayers in the temples, sacrifices, and divinations were equally useless, and were finally given up when the disaster reached overwhelming proportions. I leave all theories about its origin and its cause, if causes can be found to account for such vast disturbances, to other writers. For myself, I will describe its nature and the symptoms by which one can recognize it, if it ever breaks out again. This I can do, since I had the disease myself and also watched its course in Athens.

In general, there seemed no particular cause for coming down with the plague. Even people in good health were suddenly seized by violent fevers. The eyes became inflamed and reddened, the throat and tongue became bloody. Sneezing and hoarseness soon followed, and the disease passed to the chest producing a hard cough. Then it settled in the stomach, producing great pain and spasms. The skin was not very hot to the touch though reddish in appearance and breaking out into sores. But internally, the patients burned and couldn't stand to have any clothing at all touch them. They wanted to throw themselves into cold water and had an unquenchable thirst. In addition, the miserable feeling of never being able to rest or sleep tormented them. Strangely enough, while patients were sickest, their bodies did not waste away. It was extraordinary how the body could hold out against the attack of the disease. But on the seventh or eighth day, they died from internal inflammation even though there was still strength in them.

During the plague, Athens was not much troubled by ordinary diseases, but when someone became ill from some other cause, he eventually contracted the plague. Some died from neglect, others died in spite of intense care. No remedy or drug was ever found. What helped in one case did harm in others.

The worst feature was the dejection that occurred when anyone realized he was becoming ill. This despair immediately took away all power of resistance. Another horrible aspect was the sight of men dying like sheep, having caught the disease while nursing one another. This was particularly the case with those who had any claim to goodness. Their own honor made them nurse their friends from whom they then caught the disease and died. The sick and the dying received the most help and compassion from those few who had recovered from the plague. These knew how painful the sickness was, and they had no fear themselves, since the same person was never attacked twice. However, such people, in their excitement and elation, half-believed that they were now safe from every form of illness and misfortune.

The sacred places and temples, where many of the sick went, became full of corpses, and these remained there just as they were. As the disaster went beyond all bounds, men no longer had any idea what was to become of them. Therefore, they became completely careless about everything, whether sacred or merely human. All the burial ceremonies were abandoned, and people buried friends and relatives as best they could. And this wasn't the only form of lawless action that owed its origin to the plague. Men now did calmly and in public what previously they would only do in secret. Great changes were also brought about by constantly seeing wealthy people dying suddenly, and the poor becoming rich. All resolved to spend quickly and enjoy themselves, since they began to look at their lives and their wealth as things that wouldn't last. Honor no longer existed, and planning for the future vanished, since it was so uncertain that anyone would survive to reach a goal. Instead, immediate pleasure and everything assisting it came to be considered both honorable and useful.

The fear of the gods or of the laws of men could no longer restrain anyone. As for the gods, all Athenians judged that it was the same whether they worshiped them or not, since they saw that religious and pious people died as frequently as those who were irreligious and impious. And as for the laws of men, no one took those seriously, since no one expected to live long enough to be brought to trial for his crimes. Instead all Athenians felt that a far heavier sentence had already been passed on them and hung over their heads. And they all believed that before this sentence fell, it was only reasonable to enjoy life a little.

The Plague
by Albert Camus

The word "plague" had just been said to him for the first time. With very small differences, Dr. Rieux's reaction was the same as that of most of the people in town. Everyone knows that epidemics have a way of repeating themselves in the world, yet we find it hard to believe that they will happen to us. There have been as many epidemics in history as there have been wars, yet epidemics and wars always take people by surprise.

In fact, Dr. Rieux was caught off his guard, and we should understand that his uncertainty was due to this. He was torn between his fears and a feeling of confidence. When a war is declared, people say, "This can't last long, it's too stupid." But although a war may be stupid, that doesn't keep it from lasting. Stupidity is very insistent. We would see this if we weren't so wrapped up in ourselves.

In this respect, our townsfolk were like everybody else, wrapped up in themselves. They did not believe in epidemics. Since an epidemic is beyond our imaginations, we tell ourselves that it is a bad dream that will go away by itself. But it doesn't pass away, it is men who pass away, and first of all those who haven't taken precautions because they don't believe in epidemics.

Dr. Rieux tried to remember what he had read about the plague. Numbers floated through his memory. He remembered the thirty or so great epidemics in history that had caused a hundred million deaths. But what are a hundred million deaths? Since a dead man is not real unless you have actually seen him, a hundred million bodies spread throughout history are like a puff of smoke in the imagination. He remembered the plague at Constantinople in which ten thousand people died in one day. Ten thousand people are about five times the audience in a big theater. Yes, this is how it should be thought of. You should collect the bodies at the exits of the movie theaters. You should lead them to the city square and make them die in bunches if you wanted a clear idea of what it means. Then you should also have some familiar faces among the dead. But naturally this couldn't be put into practice. Besides, who knows ten thousand people anyway? In any case, everyone knows that these old stories about epidemics are not reliable.

The doctor made an effort to stop thinking about this. He was letting his imagination play tricks on him, and he couldn't afford it. He must fix his mind on the observed facts. All the patients who had recently died had the following symptoms: extreme weakness, delirium, swollen glands, constant thirst, dark spots on the body, and in conclusion … the doctor remembered the sentence in his medical handbook, "pulse becomes weak, and uneven, and death results when the patient makes the slightest movement." Yes, three out of four of his patients (he remembered the exact numbers) were so impatient that they made that slight movement.

Dr. Rieux was looking out of the window at a beautiful and peaceful, cool spring day. Inside his room, the word "plague" was still echoing. The word brought up in the doctor's mind not only what science had put into it, but a whole series of wild possibilities that seemed foreign to the hustle and bustle of the happy city beyond his window. The peacefulness of the town made the old descriptions of the plague seem unreal: Athens a stinking graveyard deserted even by the birds; Chinese towns filled with victims silent in their agony; the convicts at Marseilles piling corpses into pits; the damp, rotting beds stuck to the mud floor of the hospital in Constantinople, where patients were hauled from their beds with hooks; men and women making love in the cemeteries of Milan; carloads of bodies rumbling through the darkness of night in London; nights and days always and everywhere filled with the cry of human pain. No, all these horrors were not near enough to upset the peace of a spring afternoon. The comforting sounds of a streetcar came through the window. Only the sea, which he could hear beyond the town, told of the unrest and danger present in the world. The sea reminded Dr. Rieux of the fires that the Athenians lit on the seashore. The dead were brought there after dark, and since there was not enough room for everyone, the living fought one another for a space to lay the bodies of their friends and relatives. They would rather fight than let those bodies be cast into the sea. As this last image rose before his mind, he knew that it had happened, and that it could happen again.

But these wild thoughts died down as he began to think more reasonably. True, the word plague had been said, and there had been one or two victims. Still the epidemic could be stopped. It was only a question of clearly recognizing what needed to be done, and doing it. Then the plague would come to an end, because it was unthinkable that it wouldn't. If it came to an end by itself everything would be fine; if not, one would know it for what it is. Then steps could be taken for coping with and finally overcoming it.

The doctor opened the window, and at once the noises of the town grew louder. He pulled himself together. He recognized that reality lay in those everyday sounds, and not in his imaginings. All these fears about the plague were unimportant. The important thing was to do your job as it should be done.

Discussion Evaluation Form

The items below are discussion dynamics that may or may not be present in your group. Decide to what extent you think that each dynamic was present in the discussion. Then decide whether you think the group needs to work to improve in this area.

	None Some Great deal	Need to Improve?
Dominance by some individuals	1 2 3 4 5 6 7 8 9 10	Yes ❏ No ❏
Cooperation	1 2 3 4 5 6 7 8 9 10	Yes ❏ No ❏
Silence	1 2 3 4 5 6 7 8 9 10	Yes ❏ No ❏
Interrupting	1 2 3 4 5 6 7 8 9 10	Yes ❏ No ❏
Respect	1 2 3 4 5 6 7 8 9 10	Yes ❏ No ❏
Balanced participation	1 2 3 4 5 6 7 8 9 10	Yes ❏ No ❏
Active listening	1 2 3 4 5 6 7 8 9 10	Yes ❏ No ❏
Lack of interest	1 2 3 4 5 6 7 8 9 10	Yes ❏ No ❏
Asking one other questions	1 2 3 4 5 6 7 8 9 10	Yes ❏ No ❏
Building on one other's contributions	1 2 3 4 5 6 7 8 9 10	Yes ❏ No ❏
Many people talking at once	1 2 3 4 5 6 7 8 9 10	Yes ❏ No ❏

Pick one of the dynamics that you think the group should work to improve, and explain why.

How would you rate this discussion on a scale of 1–10? ___

Diversity and Factions

One of the main difficulties in creating a discussion group involves the way we selectively attend to some people over others. Feeling closer to some people than to others is perfectly natural. However, this feeling of closeness or distance often results in our responding more positively to certain members of the group than we do to others. In extreme cases, it results in our being hostile to some group members or not paying attention to them at all. When this happens, the group divides into subgroups, or factions.

Factions often form when a discussion group thinks that it is taking control of the activity. As members of the group look less to the leader and more to one another, they begin to take ownership of the process. Alliances that have existed in other arenas are sometimes brought into the discussion group at this point. Thus the emergence of factions is to be expected—but if such cliques persist, they become a serious threat to a group's ability to reach the goal of individual and collective exploration of our presuppositions and attitudes. Yet at the same time, the differences among us that factions reflect are essential to making this exploration possible.

The sources of factions are many. One driving factor is the perception of common or divergent interests—the sort of feelings that may unite people in the same profession or divide economic competitors. However, factions are also often based on common or divergent opinions and attitudes. Factions based on opinions and attitudes can stem from many sources, but usually relate to aspects of our lives that have shaped us the most profoundly—common experiences with our families and old friends, with the areas in which we have grown up, with our educational backgrounds, and with our religions. The similarities that incline us to form groups emerge most strongly when a set of important, or even fundamental, beliefs are held in common.

Although those inside our factions may be the people with whom we share the most, those outside our groups are not all equally far away. There are many people, of course, whose lives seem so different from ours that we hardly notice them. There are many ways in which we objectify and discount such people, and we must all face the challenge of how to understand the humanity of those who seem to differ from us the most radically. However, the bitterness of civil war and sectarian strife bears witness to the fact that often the strongest and most lasting antagonisms occur not among those who seem utterly foreign to one another, but among those who share some but not all their fundamental beliefs. These are the people with whom we live, study, and work. Such people can make us wonder how someone who seems to have so much "right" could be so perversely "wrong" on just the essential point. Yet it is especially such people—those with whom we partially agree and yet also essentially differ—whom we need most of all in order to form a discussion group capable of genuine exploration.

One of our goals in Touchstones is to uncover and explore our deepest presuppositions. These beliefs are the ones that are so basic to us that they seem invisible. However, these "invisible" beliefs are precisely the ones we share with others with whom we feel especially connected and close. We are close with those others because so much between us goes without saying. Yet because the things we share go without saying, we never need to say them. And when we never say them, never raise them to the surface for comment or examination, we forget their very existence. They sustain us, connect us with one another, and make us who we are, yet they generally go unnoticed. The people who can help us most in recognizing such deeply held beliefs are not those with whom we have very little in common—those with whom we have to struggle even to have a point of contact—but those with whom we share some fundamental beliefs and from whom we depart on other beliefs. These are precisely the people who are here with us, engaged in the same activity, but who are in some other subgroup. Interacting with people who share many of our presuppositions but seem to have brought them to different conclusions or to have turned them in different directions helps us recognize our own presuppositions. Curiously, the people with whom we have disagreements and agreements on a fundamental level are invaluable to us for the very task that we are jointly undertaking and to which we are all committed.

The paired texts in this volume, like factions, can help us analyze presuppositions. The texts' authors share certain attitudes and diverge on others. This divergence enables us to see and consider assumptions that are normally invisible. We must be able to attend both to these paired texts and to those people in different subgroups whom we would tend ordinarily to dismiss or confront. Through agreements and disagreements, we, like the texts, become touchstones in determining what each of us believes.

The process of group formation is mirrored in today's texts by Jean Jacques Rousseau and Sigmund Freud, both of whom postulate on the origin of civilization. Along the way, they describe the emergence of the bonds, affections, and conflicts that shape our lives with one another. Rousseau emphasizes that the preservation of one's life was the foremost concern for primitive people and that, from this concern, arose recognition of the difference between humans and animals, of the need to sometimes act toward others for the sake of safety, and of the distrust that arises in situations of competition. Conversely, the selection by Freud focuses on the roles of work and cooperation amidst the development of families. As cooperation expanded beyond families, civilizations were formed; however, the family and the larger community, Freud argues, are in conflict because the family doesn't want to give up its members to the larger society.

Worksheet 7

Rousseau and Freud each propose a theory of the origins of civilization—and with civilization, the origins of the bonds of affection and necessity that both bring us together and drive wedges between us. The unit's introduction suggests that these differences among us can become strengths as we seek to explore different perspectives. In the worksheet, we are asked to consider some of the bonds that civilization has created and how strongly we feel them to be at work in our lives and our society.

1. Below are a number of sources of bonding as well as division among people. Rate how strong a bond each source creates for you on a scale of 1 to10, with 10 meaning generally creates a very strong bond with others and 1 meaning creates a very weak bond. Then rate what you judge to be the strength of this bond more generally in society.

	You	The nation
same religion	_____	_____
same family	_____	_____
same ethnic background	_____	_____
same social class	_____	_____
same political party	_____	_____
same economic status	_____	_____
business partners	_____	_____
same position in an organization	_____	_____
same college	_____	_____
same gender	_____	_____

2. Choose one of bonds that you rated 8 or higher in respect to yourself, and suggest how you might work to form a close connection between you and someone with whom you do not share this bond.

3. Which bond do you think is the most likely to create conflicts that are hard or even impossible to overcome when it is not shared? Why?

4. After reading the texts, write an opening question for the discussion.

The Origin of Inequality among Men
by Jean Jacques Rousseau

Primitive man's first concern was to preserve his own life. The products of the earth furnished him with what he needed. His instincts showed him how to use them. Hunger and thirst and his other needs drove him to widen his experience of things in the world. There was one desire by which he was able to preserve not only his life but his species. This blind desire was at first a purely animal act and did not involve any tender feelings. When their desire was satisfied, the male and female no longer recognized each other. Even the child produced by this act no longer meant anything to the mother as soon as it could do without her.

This was the condition of primitive man. Primitive man did not know very well how to profit from the gifts of nature because he was not, at first, capable of thought. But difficulties arose, and it was necessary to learn to conquer them. Tall trees that prevented him from reaching their fruit, the competition of other animals that wanted the same fruits, and the fierceness of animals that attacked him, all forced him to become more agile, faster, and stronger. Man soon learned to use tree branches and stones as weapons. He learned to climb trees and to fight other animals. Men even learned to fight with one another. By using things such as branches and stones as tools and weapons, man began to recognize certain relationships. Those relationships are now expressed by the words "larger," "smaller," "stronger," "weaker," "faster," "slower," "more fearful," "braver," and other similar ideas.

These developments increased his superiority over other animals by making him aware of his superiority. He set traps for animals and tricked them in a thousand ways. Many animals were quicker and stronger than he was. Some of these he tamed to his own uses; the others he learned how to kill. These achievements made man proud. It made him capable of recognizing himself as different from, and superior to, the other animals.

Primitive man did not associate with his fellow men as we do. His relations with them were more like his relations with other animals. But the special intimate relations between male and female led man to recognize that other humans with whom he did not have such relations were nonetheless like him. He began to see that they all acted as he would have acted under the same circumstances. He concluded that their thoughts and feelings were like his own. This experience showed him how to act toward others for his own safety and interest.

Experience taught him that love of his own well-being is the only motive of human actions. Experience also taught him how to distinguish those rare occasions when the common interest made it possible for him to count on the help of his fellow men. It also allowed him to recognize those when competition should make him distrust them. In the first case, he united with men in a group that lasted only as long as the need lasted. In the second case, everyone tried to gain his own advantage, either by pure force or by cleverness and cunning.

The most important next advance was the construction of permanent homes. This made it possible for families to develop and to distinguish themselves from other families. The first developments of tender emotions were an effect of this new situation that united husbands and wives, parents and children. Each family became a little society in which each member was free, and all were united by mutual affection. Before this time, males and females lived in pretty much the same way. With the establishment of the family, women tended to care for home and children, while men hunted for food. Because life was easier, the two sexes began to lose their strength and aggressiveness. This made them less suited to fighting but more suited to living together.

This new way of life with its limited needs, and with the tools men had invented, allowed man large amounts of leisure. He used this leisure to acquire goods and property. These goods and property imposed the first firm limitations on man's freedom. These possessions were the first source of the evils that have since then plagued the human race. For, besides continuing to weaken their minds and bodies, these possessions stopped being luxuries, and through habit, turned into needs. Men now became unhappy at losing possessions without any longer being happy at possessing them.

Young people from different families began to associate. They began to compare themselves with one another and thus to acquire ideas of goodness and beauty. These ideas produced feelings of preference—of preferring one thing or person to another because of goodness or beauty. Tender and gentle feelings between persons began to emerge. With this emergence of love, jealousy also emerged. With jealousy, disagreements and hostilities arose. So this love, the gentlest of passions, led to the shedding of human blood.

As these new ideas and feelings appeared, the bonds between people became stronger, and thus human society grew. People grew accustomed to gathering in front of the huts or around a large tree. Song and dance, the true children of love and leisure, became the amusement of idle and assembled men and women. Each began to look at the others and to want to be looked at. Public praise began to acquire a value. The one who sang or danced the best, the handsomest, the strongest, the most agile, or the best speaker, became highly admired. This was the first step toward inequality and vice. From these first preferences were born shame and envy. When these feelings were mixed together and came into conflict, human happiness and innocence were destroyed.

Civilization and Its Discontents
by Sigmund Freud

The development of civilizations is a special process, comparable to the growth of an individual from infant to adult. Showing that this is true is an immense task. It involves discovering how civilizations began, and how the course of their development has been determined. At the present time, I have only the following speculations to offer.

After primitive man discovered that he could improve his life by working, he also discovered that it was to his advantage to cooperate with other men. Even before this, human beings adopted the habit of forming families. This was the first form of cooperation. I think that families began when the need for sexual satisfaction became continual, and not seasonal as it is with the animals. When this happened, the male had a motive for keeping the female near him. And the female was obliged in the interest of her helpless young to stay with the stronger male. But this primitive family is still not civilization because the will of its head, the father, is unrestricted. Further advance toward civilization was made when the sons of this father discovered that together they were stronger than he. However, in order to be able to cooperate, the sons had to impose restrictions on one another. These restrictions were the first laws.

The communal life of human beings originates from the necessity to work together and from the power of love. Love and necessity are also the origins of civilization. Civilization refers to a large number of people living and working together in a community. With these origins, the development of civilizations would seem to have as a result that people become happier and happier. However, this has not happened.

The love that founded the family continues to function in civilizations in both its sexual and nonsexual forms. The effect of love is to bind large numbers of people together. In fact, it does this more effectively than does the need to work together. The word "love" has many meanings in ordinary language. It means the relation between a man and a woman whose sexual needs have led them to begin a family. It also refers to the positive feelings between parents and children and between brothers and sisters. In my opinion, these latter feelings of affection began as sexual love. Both kinds of love, the sexual and nonsexual, extend outside the family and create bonds with people who used to be strangers. Sexual love leads to the formation of new families, and nonsexual love leads to the formation of friendships. Friendships are important for civilization because they are not exclusive. It is possible to be friends with many people. It would seem that love in both its forms is important for civilization, and that civilization helps to spread both sexual love and friendship. However, love and civilization come in conflict.

This conflict first expresses itself as the conflict between the family and the larger community. As I have said, one of the aims of civilization is to bring people together. However, the family is reluctant to give up its members. The more closely the members of a family are attached to one another, the more they cut themselves off from others. A tightly knit family makes it difficult for them to enter into a wider circle of life. Separating oneself from the family is a task that faces every young person. Society helps him in this task through education and the need for working with others.

Also, women, who began civilization by the claims of their love, soon came into opposition to civilization. Women represent the interest of the family and of sexual love. The work of civilization is increasingly the work of men. It confronts them with more and more difficult tasks. Since a man has only a limited amount of energy, he can accomplish these tasks only by withdrawing from women and sexual life. He has to associate constantly with other men, and this makes him neglect his duties as a father and husband.

Civilization, therefore, as it increases in size, tends also to restrict sexual life. The main reason for these restrictions is that civilization requires that people use most of their energy for work and not for pleasure. In this way, civilization treats sexual desire as if it were a potentially rebellious part of a population that needs to be suppressed. Western European civilization has done this more than other civilizations.

One of the first restrictions is the requirement that sexual partners not be of the same family. Sexuality in children is also not permitted by civilization, and there is a further requirement that the sexual life of adults must have one form. It must be heterosexual, and it must be with one person. Civilization is prepared to tolerate sexuality only because it is needed to continue the human race.

This is an extreme picture, and we know that there are many exceptions. There are so many exceptions that they have stopped being punished. But we should not assume because of this that the sexual life of civilized people is not severely restricted. It is! And the pressures from this restriction are what make the life of civilized human beings not as happy as we might have expected.

Discussion Evaluation Form

The items below are discussion dynamics that may or may not be present in your group. Decide to what extent you think that each dynamic was present in the discussion. Then decide whether you think the group needs to work to improve in this area.

	None Some Great deal	Need to Improve?
Dominance by some individuals	1 2 3 4 5 6 7 8 9 10	Yes ❑ No ❑
Cooperation	1 2 3 4 5 6 7 8 9 10	Yes ❑ No ❑
Silence	1 2 3 4 5 6 7 8 9 10	Yes ❑ No ❑
Interrupting	1 2 3 4 5 6 7 8 9 10	Yes ❑ No ❑
Respect	1 2 3 4 5 6 7 8 9 10	Yes ❑ No ❑
Balanced participation	1 2 3 4 5 6 7 8 9 10	Yes ❑ No ❑
Active listening	1 2 3 4 5 6 7 8 9 10	Yes ❑ No ❑
Lack of interest	1 2 3 4 5 6 7 8 9 10	Yes ❑ No ❑
Asking one other questions	1 2 3 4 5 6 7 8 9 10	Yes ❑ No ❑
Building on one other's contributions	1 2 3 4 5 6 7 8 9 10	Yes ❑ No ❑
Many people talking at once	1 2 3 4 5 6 7 8 9 10	Yes ❑ No ❑

Pick one of the dynamics that you think the group should work to improve, and explain why.

How would you rate this discussion on a scale of 1–10? __

8

Excluded Persons

Nothing is more destructive to a discussion group than to have some group members exclude themselves or others from participation. Although it will be somewhat rare to have everyone participate in every session, it is crucial that each person feels that his or her comments are welcomed and responded to, and feels desirous of responding to the remarks of others. When someone is just filling a chair, the effect on the group can be stultifying even if the other group members do not fully realize it. Overcoming the various forms of exclusion, either intentional or unintentional, is not something that will have already happened by the eighth or even the tenth meeting. It is a deeply ingrained habit that we will have to make continual efforts to control or perhaps eliminate. However, it is very important for the group to realize that overcoming exclusion is an essential goal on the way to being able to fully explore issues as a group. To exclude oneself or others is, in relation to the goal of probing our cultural paradigms, to leave some presuppositions and attitudes unscrutinized. A discussion group inevitably mimics our social issues and problems, so an excluded member is a sign that some important issues and concepts of our greater society—with its long history of exclusion—have not come to the surface. The reasons for group exclusions mirror the reasons for exclusions that occur in our everyday lives. These sessions therefore become the opportunity to consider such exclusions and the reasons for them without the pressure we normally face. People can exclude themselves or others for a variety of reasons that we will begin to explore.

In the first stage of *Mapping the Future*, we concentrated on the role of the leader, the use and misuse of power, and whether one needed to be an expert to participate in a discussion. Lack of expertise is one reason why people are excluded as participants and speakers. We will continue to struggle with this issue. We will never wholly dismiss the idea that, on certain topics, there are experts whose speech has a value that the nonexpert's speech lacks. The point will be for us to distinguish when such a distinction is appropriate and not simply to assume that it is always appropriate. However, beyond lack of expertise, there are other deeper and more personal reasons behind exclusion. It is these that we must now begin to examine.

It is not surprising that some people hesitate to speak in a discussion, thereby excluding themselves. We are often told that people differ from one another and that some are just naturally reticent. This might be correct in part, but it is quite rare to find someone who doesn't wish to participate because of reticence alone. Most people in discussion groups wish to participate but are blocked by other factors. We can see the desire to speak clearly when people observe or visit a discussion and are not allowed to speak. They invariably report how difficult this restriction was. Some people may refuse to participate because they are hostile to this type of activity or because they believe it isn't a real discussion—they perceive that certain answers or responses are expected. Others remain silent because they don't believe they can learn from others or because they don't think the others have fully committed to the process. These factors can look like reticence—an attitude that is often appealed to because it does not fix blame on anyone.

There are many reasons a person may hesitate to speak in a discussion even after accepting that nonexperts have something to offer and that it is possible to learn from other members of the group. One primary reason is that we may feel we should not be in doubt about what we are saying. Speech is often considered a kind of action and thus we can easily feel that we should be certain about what we say. From a certain perspective, it is perfectly reasonable that one should not wish to feel doubt about what one is stating. Part of this attitude is commendable and stems from a type of responsibility we feel or should feel toward others. We don't want to mislead them or waste their time. However, we must realize that a discussion is an exploration and is premised on the fact that the direction and approach to a topic are doubtful. It is usually those who feel uncertain who are most helpful because they are most fully aware of the uncertainty the group should feel. Participating responsibly while feeling uncertain should be a model for other members of the group. Another factor that frequently discourages people from speaking is that certain people in the group are dominant and seem to think they must respond to everything that is said. This means that if others wish to speak, dominant individuals will intervene and we will find our remarks mediated by them. Or, there might be people who love to play devil's advocate and who will hold onto a point or an opinion regardless of the course of the discussion. It is frustrating to feel that one is in a tug of war and that there is no point in trying to change a person's mind. We may exclude ourselves because we have no confidence that our words could possibly have any effect.

However, we may also be reluctant to speak because we perceive that others exclude us. A discussion format is an uncertain environment. If we speak, we cannot guarantee that we will be understood or that if we are understood, we will be taken seriously. Even worse, we may worry that someone may gratuitously attack us, or that no one will respond at all. We may fear being treated with the kind of invisibility that Ellison describes in the selection from *The Invisible Man.*

We exclude others for many reasons. We might feel they have nothing to offer because we disagree with them. We might exclude individuals because of the attitudes we bring into the meetings from our previous professional or personal relations with them. We might exclude people because they have behaved in ways that were hostile or counterproductive or because they themselves have been excluding others. Or we might exclude someone because we think the person does not listen to others or because the person has an agenda that makes him or her misread texts or misunderstand even the most clearly stated opinions. The group might genuinely be trying to correct certain members by refusing to acknowledge them. However, a discussion group should not allow itself the kind of option all too often used in our society. Rather, the group should learn to deal with its problems openly and correct itself.

The texts for this session focus on these issues of exclusion, although they approach it from different directions. The piece by Wollstonecraft views exclusion through the sense that many people have that an opinion is correct simply because they hold it or because it fits so well with their lives and their society. Such people do not allow or appreciate that others have a right to ask for reasons or evidence. They think that their own will justifies what they believe irrespective of others. The Ellison excerpt looks at the social and historical categories through which we view others and the world. It investigates how this perspective causes us to really see only ourselves and to impose ourselves on others. We exclude others by not recognizing who they are. The worksheet helps us confront our thinking about why exclusion occurs.

Worksheet 8

The texts remind us of the ways in which our society has systematically excluded women and African Americans. The introduction to Unit 8 asks us to recognize the prejudices that are at work in our own discussion group—the perhaps subtle ways in which some members of the group find their contributions discounted and become in effect invisible. Below, we are asked to consider some reasons why a person might choose not to take part in a discussion and how hard these various barriers to participation may be to overcome.

1. Listed below are ten reasons why someone might not participate in a discussion. In the first column, rank them from 1 (easiest to overcome) to 10 (hardest to overcome) as you think they apply to most people. Then in column 2, rank them as they apply to you.

	Most People	Me
a) When I speak, no one picks up on what I say.	_____	_____
b) The leader never makes eye contact with me.	_____	_____
c) One or a few people generally attack what I say.	_____	_____
d) The group never considers topics that I consider important.	_____	_____
e) The leader always agrees with a few other participants.	_____	_____
f) The discussion is never genuinely exploratory; certain group members impose an agenda.	_____	_____
g) There are a number of people I do not respect in the group.	_____	_____
h) A few others always comment on everything that is said.	_____	_____
i) People don't give reasons for their ideas.	_____	_____
j) The discussion veers all over the place and we have no direction.	_____	_____

2. Consider the items you ranked 9 and 10 for most people. What advice would you give someone to help him or her participate in spite of that problem?

3. Which items did you rank the highest for yourself?

4. After reading the texts, write an opening question.

A Vindication of the Rights of Women
by Mary Wollstonecraft

Mental activity, like bodily activity, is at first difficult and unpleasant. Therefore, many people let others both work and think for them. When in a group, a person asserts an opinion with great heat, very often it is a prejudice. Generally such a person has a high respect for the understanding of some relative or friend without fully understanding the opinions that he is now so eager to have us also believe. Therefore, he holds these opinions with a degree of force that would surprise even the person who held them in the first place.

It is now fashionable to respect prejudices. When we dare to face our prejudices, motivated by feelings of humanity and armed with reason, we are often asked whether our ancestors, who created these opinions, were fools. I reply that they weren't. Our ancestors' opinions were all probably thought about and based on some reason. But often the reason they had was special and useful only at that time. It was not a fundamental principle that would be reasonable at all times.

Our ancestors' old and moss-covered opinions become prejudices when we lazily accept them only because these opinions have been with us for a long time. An opinion is a prejudice when it is one that we like and hold strongly, but for which we can give no reason. The moment a reason can be given for an opinion it stops being a prejudice, though it may still be a mistake or an error. This way of arguing, if we can call it arguing, reminds me of what is crudely and vulgarly called 'a woman's reason.' For women sometimes say they love someone or believe certain things just because they love or believe them, and they can't or won't give any reasons.

It is useless to talk with people who only use affirmatives and negatives, who say either yes or no to everything. Before you can bring yourself or someone else to a point where you can begin a useful discussion, you must go back to the simple principles that precede the prejudices. And it is ten-to-one that you will be stopped as you try to do this. You even will be told that, though these simple principles are true in theory, they are false in practice. When you hear this from people, you may infer that their reason has whispered some doubts to them. For it generally happens that people assert their opinions with the greatest heat when they begin to waver and have doubts about them. They then try to drive out their own doubts by convincing their opponents and grow angry when their own doubts continue to bother and haunt them.

The Invisible Man
by Ralph Ellison

I am an invisible man. No, I am not a spook like those who haunted Edgar Allan Poe, nor am I one of your Hollywood-movie ectoplasms. I am a man of substance, of flesh and bone, fiber and liquids—and I might even be said to possess a mind. I am invisible, understand, simply because people refuse to see me. Like the bodiless heads you see sometimes in circus sideshows, it is as though I have been surrounded by mirrors of hard, distorting glass. When they approach me, they see only my surroundings, themselves, or figments of their imagination—indeed, everything and anything except me.

Nor is my invisibility exactly a matter of a biochemical accident to my epidermis. That invisibility to which I refer occurs because of a peculiar disposition of the eyes of those with whom I come in contact. A matter of the construction of their inner eyes, those eyes with which they look through their physical eyes upon reality. I am not complaining, nor am I protesting either. It is sometimes advantageous to be unseen, although it is most often rather wearing on the nerves. Then too, you're constantly being bumped against by those of poor vision. Or again, you often doubt if you really exist. You wonder whether you aren't simply a phantom in other people's minds. Say, a figure in a nightmare that the sleeper tries with all his strength to destroy. It's when you feel like this that, out of resentment, you begin to bump people back. And, let me confess, you feel that way most of the time. You ache with the need to convince yourself that you do exist in the real world, that you're a part of all the sounds and anguish, and you strike out with your fists, you curse, and you swear to make them recognize you. And, alas, it's seldom successful.

One night I accidentally bumped into a man, and, perhaps because of the near darkness, he saw me and called me an insulting name. I sprang at him, seized his coat lapels and demanded that he apologize. He was a tall blond man, and as my face came close to his he looked insolently out of his blue eyes and cursed me, his breath hot in my face as he struggled. I pulled his chin down sharp upon the crown of my head, butting him as I had seen the West Indians do, and I felt his flesh tear and the blood gush out, and I yelled, "Apologize! Apologize!" But he continued to curse and struggle, and I butted him again and again until he went down heavily, on his knees, profusely bleeding. I kicked him repeatedly, in a frenzy because he still uttered insults though his lips were frothy with blood. Oh yes, I kicked him! And in my outrage I got out my knife and prepared to slit his throat, right there beneath the lamplight in the deserted street, holding him in the collar with one hand, and opening the knife with my teeth—when it occurred to me that the man had not seen me, actually; that he, as far as he knew, was in the midst of a walking nightmare! And I stopped the blade, slicing the air as I pushed him away, letting him fall back to the street. I stared at him hard as the lights of a car stabbed through the darkness. He lay there, moaning on the asphalt; a man almost killed by a phantom. It unnerved me. I was both disgusted and ashamed. I was like a drunken man myself, wavering about on weakened legs. Then I was amused: something in this man's thick head had sprung out and beaten him within an inch of his life. I began to laugh at this crazy discovery. Would he have awakened at the point of death? Would Death himself have freed him for wakeful living? But I didn't linger, I ran away into the dark, laughing so hard I feared I might rupture myself.

The next day I saw his picture in the *Daily News*, beneath a caption stating that he had been "mugged." Poor fool, poor blind fool, I thought with sincere compassion, mugged by an invisible man!

Discussion Evaluation Form

The items below are discussion dynamics that may or may not be present in your group. Decide to what extent you think that each dynamic was present in the discussion. Then decide whether you think the group needs to work to improve in this area.

	None Some Great deal	Need to Improve?
Dominance by some individuals	1 2 3 4 5 6 7 8 9 10	Yes ❑ No ❑
Cooperation	1 2 3 4 5 6 7 8 9 10	Yes ❑ No ❑
Silence	1 2 3 4 5 6 7 8 9 10	Yes ❑ No ❑
Interrupting	1 2 3 4 5 6 7 8 9 10	Yes ❑ No ❑
Respect	1 2 3 4 5 6 7 8 9 10	Yes ❑ No ❑
Balanced participation	1 2 3 4 5 6 7 8 9 10	Yes ❑ No ❑
Active listening	1 2 3 4 5 6 7 8 9 10	Yes ❑ No ❑
Lack of interest	1 2 3 4 5 6 7 8 9 10	Yes ❑ No ❑
Asking one other questions	1 2 3 4 5 6 7 8 9 10	Yes ❑ No ❑
Building on one other's contributions	1 2 3 4 5 6 7 8 9 10	Yes ❑ No ❑
Many people talking at once	1 2 3 4 5 6 7 8 9 10	Yes ❑ No ❑

Pick one of the dynamics that you think the group should work to improve, and explain why.

How would you rate this discussion on a scale of 1–10? _____

Judging Others and Judging Ourselves

Throughout the program, we have been considering our attitudes about knowledge and power, both those attitudes that we have as individuals and those that characterize us as a discussion group. We have also started to look at the motives involved in the ways people behave in a discussion. For instance, when someone acts dominantly, we may judge him or her to be seizing power. However, that person might describe that same behavior quite differently. That person could claim to have been acting for the good of the group. In this example, we see certain evidence and infer a motive. The other person tells us what his or her motive is, and this conflicts with what we inferred. Each of these judgments is important, and each might contain some truth. However, the judgments are different. One is a judgment made about another person, the other is a judgment or a claim the person makes about himself or herself.

A crucial step on the way to forming a discussion group is to bring these two judgments or opinions closer together. The ways others view us and the ways we view ourselves will never be the same, and we wouldn't want them to be. None of us is transparent. Each of us remains an individual within the group, fully capable of surprising others and sometimes even ourselves. In fact, the success of the group depends on its ability to draw on the unique and often unsuspected strengths of each of its members. However, we must become aware of the two forms of judgments and be able to recognize when we are operating within one rather than another.

Furthermore, we need to learn how to shift from one viewpoint to another. This transition can often be very difficult because although our viewpoint about another person may appear to us to be precisely that—a point of view—our description of ourselves is likely to appear to us not as a point of view but as an obvious truth. This difficulty of reconciling how others see us and how we see ourselves is common to individuals, groups, organizations, and cultures. It can also be the source of terrible self-deception.

One concept used to attempt to articulate this difficulty is that of perspective. It is claimed that our understanding of another person and that person's understanding of himself or herself differ because we have different perspectives. This use of the term "perspective" refers to the idea that our physical position will determine what we see and how we see it. However, the usefulness of this concept of perspective is limited for the situation we are considering in this unit. Referring to perspective or point of view helps when both parties are considering a third object, event, or person. In the case of visual perspective, we are outside the objects we see and our position, relative to those objects, determines what we see. In looking at others and ourselves, however, the real difficulty is not that two people have different perspectives on some third external object or event. Rather, it lies in the fact that there is a difference between the way we judge others and the way we judge ourselves. We can have a perspective on another person, but what does it mean to claim we understand or describe ourselves from a certain perspective or point of view? We are not outside ourselves; we *are* ourselves. Yet for us to change requires that we look at ourselves as if we were outside ourselves.

Changing ourselves, or at least seeing ourselves and our beliefs more clearly so that we can change if we so choose, is an important goal of our exploration together. The beliefs we have been considering and will consider are indeed among those that stand at the center of our society. Recently this worldview has been referred to as a "box" in which, to a certain extent, we are held captive. People wish to learn to "think outside the box." This should not be taken to imply that our goal is to surrender all our beliefs about how the world works but rather that, for the sake of thinking more clearly, we hope to be able to see these beliefs from a different perspective. To use a different analogy, we might want to look for a moment *at* the glasses we are wearing rather than always looking *through* them. By trying on different ways of seeing, we may become more aware of how the lenses we regularly look through influence what we perceive. Such a task seems very abstract when we read about it. However, in the discussion format we approach the text in two important ways. We explore our beliefs intellectually as we think about the texts and the issues raised by the other members of our group. We also experience the tension that is created as we bring our views about the world into the conversation with others. Furthermore we find that some of the most central beliefs of our culture, those that make us who we are, are the very ones we must modify to form a successful discussion group. Identifying these assumptions and the ways in which they have shaped us and working to develop alternative ways of interacting with one another give concrete meaning to what would otherwise remain an academic exercise.

The paintings by Vermeer and Mondrian, which are this unit's texts, can assist us in this effort. We generally allow many different judgments of a painting, as opposed to texts or other areas, without disagreements arising. This allowance is frequently justified by claiming that our attitudes toward art are matters of taste and that agreement can no more be expected here than in questions about selecting our favorite foods. Thus, the expectation might be that in a discussion, we wouldn't come to any consensus about the paintings. However, paintings do often lead to extremely exploratory and cooperative discussions and, as a result of that openness and cooperation, there are many times when the participants eventually reach general agreement about the works. Discussions of art also often allow the participants to draw on different strengths than those they most often bring to the group and to see their own and others' participation in a new light. Therefore, looking at the differences between this discussion and some of your other sessions can be a fruitful entry into the issue of how we make judgments about ourselves and others.

Worksheet 9

The unit's introduction raises the issue of the presuppositions that shape our various views of the world. We see evidence of these in, for instance, the different perspectives with which we approach common experiences and the difference between the way we judge others and the way we judge ourselves. Paintings are often useful for our exploration of these issues because they are a type of "text" about which people feel freer to express the variety of their opinions without the fear of being labeled right or wrong. And this more open attitude also frees us to see how the examination of the perspectives of others both enriches us and enables us to better understand our point of view. The worksheet asks us to think about and compare (if possible) the judgments we make about ourselves with those our group makes about us.

1. Listed below are some descriptions of how people act in a discussion. Ask yourself which of these you think describes your participation. Then ask yourself which of these the other members of the group would consider to be descriptive of your participation. Put check marks in the appropriate boxes.

	How you describe yourself	How others describe you
a) You listen carefully to others.	❏	❏
b) You don't argue for the sake of arguing.	❏	❏
c) You participate a responsible amount.	❏	❏
d) You are interested in hearing new points of view.	❏	❏
e) You try to help the sessions succeed.	❏	❏
f) You are willing to change your mind.	❏	❏
g) You ask helpful questions.	❏	❏
h) You help others explain their ideas.	❏	❏
i) You build on what others say.	❏	❏
j) You raise useful questions and topics.	❏	❏

2. Choose one of the above descriptions for which you believe there to be a difference in how you see your own participation and how others see it, and briefly explain the difference of judgment.

3. Write an opening question for the discussion.

Woman Holding a Balance
by Johannes Vermeer

and

Diamond Painting in Red, Yellow, and Blue
by Piet Mondrian

The paintings can be found in the back of the book on pages 228 and 229.

Discussion Evaluation Form

The items below are discussion dynamics that may or may not be present in your group. Decide to what extent you think that each dynamic was present in the discussion. Then decide whether you think the group needs to work to improve in this area.

	None Some Great deal	Need to Improve?
Dominance by some individuals	1 2 3 4 5 6 7 8 9 10	Yes ❏ No ❏
Cooperation	1 2 3 4 5 6 7 8 9 10	Yes ❏ No ❏
Silence	1 2 3 4 5 6 7 8 9 10	Yes ❏ No ❏
Interrupting	1 2 3 4 5 6 7 8 9 10	Yes ❏ No ❏
Respect	1 2 3 4 5 6 7 8 9 10	Yes ❏ No ❏
Balanced participation	1 2 3 4 5 6 7 8 9 10	Yes ❏ No ❏
Active listening	1 2 3 4 5 6 7 8 9 10	Yes ❏ No ❏
Lack of interest	1 2 3 4 5 6 7 8 9 10	Yes ❏ No ❏
Asking one other questions	1 2 3 4 5 6 7 8 9 10	Yes ❏ No ❏
Building on one other's contributions	1 2 3 4 5 6 7 8 9 10	Yes ❏ No ❏
Many people talking at once	1 2 3 4 5 6 7 8 9 10	Yes ❏ No ❏

Pick one of the dynamics that you think the group should work to improve, and explain why.

How would you rate this discussion on a scale of 1–10? _____

Self-Examination

This session is the midway point in *Mapping the Future* and an appropriate time to take stock of our progress. In the first stage of this program, we moved from expecting the leader to direct our efforts to expecting to be co-explorers in the discussion. The leader, we found, was not the source of expertise or additional information but instead was the conscience of the group—the person who kept us on task and encouraged each of us to take greater initiative. To find answers, we needed to work together.

This focus on cooperation meant that we all had to start taking responsibility for the direction of the investigation in each session. Over the last few sessions of the second stage, we have sought to enable each member of the group to voice his or her own experiences and thoughts. We have also sought to break down factions or subgroups that could lead to many "leaders" vying for control. In many respects, we have formed a discussion group. There are certainly still problems to face and overcome, but much has been accomplished. In particular, we (a) now speak directly with one another and not through the leader, (b) are willing to risk being mistaken and to admit when we are wrong, (c) can ask for assistance from others without feeling embarrassed that we have failed, (d) don't cling dogmatically to a point that we are making, and (e) don't expect that we will cover a set program of material in our sessions and come to closure. All these accomplishments are important milestones in our group's evolution.

As the group has evolved, we have created and modeled new patterns of behavior. A discussion group is an ideal way to experiment with new varieties of cooperation and organizational structure. Within the context of the group, we are able to experience the initial confusion that occurs when we relinquish traditional hierarchical structures as well as the emergence of cooperative problem-solving and the beginnings of truly shared leadership. As we practice examining complex and challenging ideas together, we find ourselves modeling the very types of approaches that are particularly useful in modern workplaces and daily life.

To facilitate the task of examining our discussion group, let us return to a topic we considered in Unit 6: the distinction we usually make between the attitudes we believe should govern our lives in the public realm and those we believe ought to be dominant in the private sphere. The following are ways in which our expectations in these arenas may differ.

Values traditionally characteristic of the public realm:

- Objectivity
- A critical and skeptical manner
- Efficiency
- The idea that problems have definite solutions
- Expertise and professionalism
- Maintenance of organizational hierarchy
- Control
- Minimization of risk

Values traditionally characteristic of the private, or personal, realm:

- Subjectivity
- Trust
- Spontaneity
- Compromise
- Self-expression
- Fluidity
- Openness
- Risk as important for growth

In taking stock of our progress, we will examine the development of our group through the paradigm given to us in these pairs of opposed values. We will also consider whether in developing new forms of behavior, we are changing our attitudes and expectations in these areas.

Both texts for in this unit were written to bring others to an attitude of self-examination. In the first text, Frederick Douglass attempts to get a nation to think seriously about slavery. He does this indirectly by writing a public letter to his former master, highlighting the abstract question of slavery by focusing on his own experience and the plight he imagines his family to be enduring. Since it is unlikely that his former master would have read this letter, it can be read as if addressed to all potential readers. However, other readers can use the specific addressee, Thomas Auld, to create distance between themselves and the person being criticized in the letter. This distance allows readers to examine their own attitudes and behavior without feeling as if they are being personally attacked. The general issue of slavery is viewed within the particular context of the destruction of the writer's own family.

The piece by Mohandas K. Gandhi takes a different direction. It discusses "satyagraha." Gandhi claims that the word is untranslatable, although it is often inadequately translated to mean "passive resistance." It is a type of resistance that is far from passive, even though it may appear as if those practicing it are not doing anything. Satyagraha is a posture toward our aggressors in which we resist not the suffering inflicted on us but the urge to respond to such suffering. Great discipline, effort, and activity are required to overcome the desire to respond. What is meant to happen is that in refusing to defend oneself or respond to the attack, one renders the perpetrators' actions visible to them. This is a different approach to guiding an individual or a group toward self-examination. We might ask how, in the development of our group or in other experiences we may have, our own actions and presuppositions may become more visible to us.

Worksheet 10

The texts by Douglass and Gandhi both concern the effort to bring others—in these cases oppressors—to self-examination. How does one induce other people or groups to examine and perhaps reevaluate their own behavior? The introduction asks us to examine our progress as a discussion group and the challenges that remain to be met. As we assess the development of our group, we must ask ourselves about the goals toward which we are working. The worksheet gives us the opportunity to make explicit our intuitions about what ought most ideally to characterize our discussions together.

1. Listed below are pairs of beliefs that underlie our behavior in our public and private lives. Consider the traits that you think should, ideally, characterize a discussion. Then divide up 10 points between the items of the pair, allocating points to indicate the relative value of the attitudes within the context of an ideal discussion. For instance, considering efficiency and spontaneity, one might think that it is important for our discussions to move along effectively, but still more important that our discussions go where the process leads us without rigid control. So one might give efficiency a 3, spontaneity a 7. Another person might think that a discussion requires more attempts to reach a conclusion and give efficiency a 6 and spontaneity a 4.

Characteristics of an Ideal Discussion

a) _____ Objectivity

_____ Subjectivity

10

b) _____ Skepticism

_____ Trust

10

c) _____ Efficiency

_____ Spontaneity

10

d) _____ Problems have definite

solutions

_____ Problems have several

plausible solutions

10

e) _____ Individuality and creativity

_____ Professionalism and expert

knowledge

10

f) _____ Structure

_____ Flexibility

10

g) _____ Situations should be controlled   h) _____ Risk aversion

_____ Openness to new situations   _____ Risk taking

10   10

2. After reading the texts, write *two* opening questions—one for a discussion starting with the piece by Douglass and one for a discussion starting with the piece by Gandhi.

Letter to His Former Master
by Frederick Douglass

Thomas Auld:

Sir—The long and intimate, though by no means friendly, relation that unhappily existed between you and myself, leads me to hope that you will easily account for the great liberty that I now take in addressing you in this open and public manner. The same fact may possibly remove any disagreeable surprise that you may experience on again finding your name coupled with mine in any other way than in an advertisement accurately describing my person and offering a large sum for my arrest. In thus dragging you again before the public, I am aware that I shall subject myself to no small amount of blame. I shall probably be charged with unwarrantable, if not a wanton and reckless, disregard of the rights and properties of private life. There are those North as well as South who entertain a much higher respect for rights that are merely conventional than they do for rights that are personal and essential.

I have selected this day on which to address you because it is the anniversary of my emancipation; and knowing of no better way, I am led to this as the best mode of celebrating that truly important event. Just ten years ago this beautiful September morning, yon bright sun beheld me a slave—a poor, degraded chattel—trembling at the sound of your voice, lamenting that I was a man, and wishing myself a brute. You, sir, can never know my feelings. As I look back to them, I can scarcely realize that I have passed through a scene so trying.

Oh! Sir, a slaveholder never appears to me so completely an agent of hell as when I think of, and look upon, my dear children. It is then that my feelings rise above my control. I meant to have said more with respect to my own prosperity and happiness, but thoughts and feelings which this recital has awakened unfit me to proceed further in that direction—the grim direction! The grim horrors of slavery rise in all their ghastly terror before me, the wails of millions pierce my heart, and chill my blood. I remember the chain, the gag, the bloody whip, the death-like gloom overshadowing the broken spirit of the fettered bondman, the appalling liability of his being torn away from wife and children and sold like a beast in the market. Say not that this is a picture of fancy. You well know that I carry scars on my back inflicted by your instruction, and that you, while we were brothers in the same church, caused this right hand, with which I am now penning this letter, to be closely tied to my left and my person dragged at the pistol's mouth for fifteen miles from the Bay side to Easton to be sold like a beast in the market for the alleged crime of intending to escape from your possession. All this and more you remember and know to be perfectly true, not only of yourself but of nearly all of the slaveholders around you.

At this moment, you are probably the guilty holder of at least three of my own dear sisters and my only brother in bondage. These you regard as your property. They are recorded on your ledger and perhaps are still filling your own ever-hungry purse by their work. Sir, I desire to know how and where these dear sisters are. Let me know all about them. I would write to them and learn all I want to know of them without disturbing you in any way, but that, through your unrighteous conduct, they have been entirely deprived of the power to read and write. You have kept them in utter ignorance and have therefore robbed them of the sweet enjoyments of writing or receiving letters from absent friends and relatives. Your wickedness and cruelty committed in this respect on your fellow creatures are greater than all the blows you have laid upon my back or theirs. It is an outrage upon the soul—a war upon the immortal spirit, and one for which you must give account at the bar of our common Father and Creator.

I will now bring this letter to a close; you shall hear from me again unless you let me hear from you. I intend to make use of you as a weapon with which to assail the system of slavery—as a means of concentrating public attention on the system and deepening their horror of trafficking in the souls and bodies of men. I shall make use of you as a means of bringing this guilty nation with yourself to repentance. In doing this, I entertain no malice toward you personally. There is no roof under which you would be safer than mine, and there is nothing in my house that you might need for your comfort that I would not readily grant. Indeed, I should esteem it a privilege to set you an example as to how mankind ought to treat each other.

I am your fellow man, but not your slave.
Frederick Douglass

Writings on Nonviolence from Young India 1920

by Mohandas K. Gandhi

Satyagraha

For the past 30 years in my social actions, I have been preaching and practicing Satyagraha, which is often imperfectly translated as "nonviolence." The principles of Satyagraha, as I know it today, have evolved gradually. Satyagraha differs from Passive Resistance as the North Pole from the South. Passive Resistance has been conceived as a weapon of the weak and does not exclude the use of physical force or violence for the purpose of gaining one's end. Satyagraha, on the other hand, has been conceived as a weapon of the strongest and excludes the use of violence in any shape or form.

Its root meaning is 'holding on to truth,' hence Truth-force. I have also called it Love-force or Soul-force. In the application of Satyagraha, I discovered in the early stages that the pursuit of truth did not admit of violence being inflicted on one's opponent, but that he must be weaned from error by patience and sympathy. For what appears to be truth to the one may appear to be error to the other. And patience means self-suffering. So the doctrine came to mean persuading another of truth not by infliction of suffering on the opponent but on one's self.

But on the political field the struggle on behalf of the people mostly consists of opposing error in the shape of unjust laws. When you have failed to bring the error home to the lawgiver by way of petitions and the like, the only remedy open to you, if you do not wish to submit to error, is to compel him by physical force to yield to you or by suffering in your own person by inviting the penalty for breaking the law. Hence, Satyagraha largely appears to the public as Civil Disobedience or Civil Resistance. It is civil in the sense that it is not criminal.

The criminal lawbreaker breaks the law surreptitiously or secretly and tries to avoid the penalty; not so with the civil resister. He always obeys the laws of the State to which he belongs, not out of fear of the sanctions but because he considers them to be good for the welfare of society. But there come occasions, generally rare, when he considers certain laws to be so unjust as to render obedience to them a dishonor. He then openly and civilly breaks them and quietly suffers the penalty for their breach.

In my opinion, the beauty and efficacy of Satyagraha is so great and the doctrine so simple that it can be preached even to children. It was preached by me with excellent results to thousands of Indian men, women, and children commonly called indentured servants.

Domestic Satyagraha

I had read in some books on vegetarianism that salt was not a necessary food for man, that on the contrary, a salt-less diet was better for health. I had deduced that a brahmarchari, or a person who strives for complete control of the senses, benefited by a salt-less diet. I had also read and realized that the weak-bodied should avoid beans and lentils of which I was very fond. Now it happened that Kasturba, my wife, who had a brief period of relief after an operation, had again begun hemorrhaging and the problem would not improve. Hydropathic treatment by itself did not answer. Kasturba had not much faith in my remedies, though she did not resist them. She certainly did not ask for outside help. So when all my remedies had failed, I entreated her to give up salt, beans, and lentils. She would not agree, however much I pleaded with her, though I supported myself with authorities. At last, she challenged me saying that even I could not give up these foods if I was advised to do so. I was pained and equally delighted—delighted in that I got an opportunity to shower my love on her. I said to her, "You are mistaken. If I were ailing and the doctor advised me to give up these or other foods, I should unhesitatingly do so. But there! Without any medical advice, I give up salt, beans, and lentils for one year, whether you do so or not."

She was rudely shocked and exclaimed in a deep sorrow, "Pray forgive me. Knowing you, I should not have provoked you. I promise not to eat these things, but for heaven's sake, take back your vow. Your action is too hard on me."

I replied, "It is very good for you to give up these foods. I have not the slightest doubt that you will be all the better without them. As for me, I cannot take back a vow seriously given. And it is sure to benefit me, for all restraint, whatever prompts it, is wholesome for man. You will therefore leave me alone. It will be a test for me and a moral support to you in carrying out your resolve."

So she gave up on me. "You are too obstinate. You will listen to no one," she said, and sought relief in tears.

I would like to count this incident as an instance of Satyagraha and as one of the sweetest recollections of my life.

Medically, there may be two opinions as to the value of such a diet, but morally I have no doubt that all self-denial is good for the soul. The diet of a man of self-restraint must be different from that of a man of pleasure, just as their ways of life are different.

Discussion Evaluation Form

The items below are discussion dynamics that may or may not be present in your group. Decide to what extent you think that each dynamic was present in the discussion. Then decide whether you think the group needs to work to improve in this area.

	None Some Great deal	Need to Improve?
Dominance by some individuals	1 2 3 4 5 6 7 8 9 10	Yes ❏ No ❏
Cooperation	1 2 3 4 5 6 7 8 9 10	Yes ❏ No ❏
Silence	1 2 3 4 5 6 7 8 9 10	Yes ❏ No ❏
Interrupting	1 2 3 4 5 6 7 8 9 10	Yes ❏ No ❏
Respect	1 2 3 4 5 6 7 8 9 10	Yes ❏ No ❏
Balanced participation	1 2 3 4 5 6 7 8 9 10	Yes ❏ No ❏
Active listening	1 2 3 4 5 6 7 8 9 10	Yes ❏ No ❏
Lack of interest	1 2 3 4 5 6 7 8 9 10	Yes ❏ No ❏
Asking one other questions	1 2 3 4 5 6 7 8 9 10	Yes ❏ No ❏
Building on one other's contributions	1 2 3 4 5 6 7 8 9 10	Yes ❏ No ❏
Many people talking at once	1 2 3 4 5 6 7 8 9 10	Yes ❏ No ❏

Pick one of the dynamics that you think the group should work to improve, and explain why.

How would you rate this discussion on a scale of 1–10? _____

Participant Questionnaire

In the best discussions, each person acts simultaneously as a participant and a leader. Furthermore, each group member acts with the interests of the group in mind and governs his or her participation accordingly. This self-evaluation form helps you reflect on your participation and recognize areas in which you would like to improve.

How much would you say that you participate?

❑ Less than most   ❑ About average   ❑ More than most

How often do you interrupt others?

❑ Very Little   ❑ Sometimes   ❑ Often   ❑ All the time

How often do you listen to all the participants?

❑ Very Little   ❑ Sometimes   ❑ Often   ❑ All the time

How often do you solicit other opinions?

❑ Very Little   ❑ Sometimes   ❑ Often   ❑ All the time

How often do you build on what others say?

❑ Very Little   ❑ Sometimes   ❑ Often   ❑ All the time

How often do you keep focused and on task?

❑ Very Little   ❑ Sometimes   ❑ Often   ❑ All the time

How often do you encourage quieter participants to speak?

❑ Very Little   ❑ Sometimes   ❑ Often   ❑ All the time

How often do you prepare well for the sessions?

❑ Very Little   ❑ Sometimes   ❑ Often   ❑ All the time

What is one way in which you have improved as a participant?

Name one way that you would like to improve as a participant.

Stage 3

Listening and Understanding

Recognizing Our Assumptions

Listening is an activity. It is not something that just happens; it requires our effort. How often have we been told that we haven't really heard, or understood, what someone was saying? This lack of understanding can happen simply because we weren't paying attention. Probably more frequently, however, it happens because, although we thought we were paying attention, we heard only what we wanted or expected to hear. In this stage, we will work on controlling our tendency to impose our expectations on others. We will examine our assumptions and biases, and in the process, become better able to truly listen.

This third stage of the program will last through Unit 15. The first stage, Units 1 through 5, dealt with issues of power, control, and expertise. The second stage, Units 6 through 10, focused on dominance and silence within the group and group processes and diversity. This third stage will concentrate on our ability to step outside ourselves and hear what another person is saying or discern what an author has written. Although these stages are presented distinctly, the different issues and the skills involved interpenetrate. We don't master one skill before tackling another. For instance, in the first two stages, we were already dealing with assumptions and biases even though we don't focus in depth on those issues until Stage 3. And while addressing presuppositions and the effects they have on our worldview in this third stage, we will continue to refine areas we focused on in the first two stages, particularly the way the group works together and our ideas of authority and integrity.

As we attempt to become more aware of our own assumptions and the ways in which they shape our comprehension of the world, it may be helpful to consider our stages of development in more detail. The stages of forming a group capable of genuine discussion, it turns out, mirror the evolution of philosophical thinking in Western culture. For example, we learned in the first stage that to hold a discussion, we must confront issues of authority and expertise. Our attitudes about these issues are rooted to a certain extent in the Old Testament and principally in the writings of Aristotle. As we struggled with these issues in our group, the attitudes and presuppositions underlying them became clearer to us. In the second stage, we began to consider various issues regarding the self, including diversity, exclusion, and public and private realms of behavior. We inherited this perspective on the self from the Christian tradition, in which the problem of the self deals with the nature of our will and how we often behave in ways that are opposed to the community. As we considered these issues and looked more closely at our interactions with one another, we became more aware of the unspoken attitudes that had been shaping our relations. This third stage brings us closer to the modern conception of the self, a concept that has more to do with our thinking than with our actions and wills. Here, we hope to gain new insight into the ways our patterns of thought impose on the world around us.

As we delve into this exploration, it may be helpful to understand a few general aspects of this modern conception of the self and its relationship to issues of listening.

From the early years of the Christian era through the Renaissance, the problem of the self—selfishness and self-involvement—was framed primarily as a function of our desires or willfulness. We isolated ourselves from others because of pride or despair. Starting with what we call the scientific revolution, our philosophical understanding of ourselves began to shift. What had been viewed as a problem of willfulness became more and more associated with intellectual error. This way of thinking was definitively articulated in the works of René Descartes and his intellectual descendants. Error in this context is not primarily a result of desire but rather of false beliefs. Such intellectual error often occurs when we impose our own preconceived understanding of the world on our current experience. This error is what happens when we hear or see what we expect to hear or see rather than what is actually presented to us. The intellectual movement initiated by Descartes and Galileo toward the scientific approach to seeing the world was in part an effort to create procedures that would correct our general tendency to impose our expectations onto the world.

This philosophical concern with intellectual error led to further investigation. Thinkers began to ask where we had gotten these false beliefs in the first place. If we wished to understand and control how these ideas interfered with our exploration of nature, we needed to take stock of their sources. Some of these false ideas, some philosophers held, came from our education, whereas others came from our senses and still others came from rumors or other things we heard.

However, as this issue was pursued further, a new question arose that to a large extent transcended the categories of true and false. Did all our ideas and concepts come to us from external sources or were there some that we supplied? Were we born with these ideas or were they part of the very structure of our thinking? The first person to explore this approach extensively, following the impetus of John Locke and David Hume, was the philosopher Immanuel Kant. Kant held that not all our concepts could have come from experience because some understandings—such as causality—had to already be in place for us to be able to judge that we had experienced anything at all. These concepts and ideas were neither true nor false but rather necessary for us to live in the world. They could be considered to be like a framework within which particular events could be experienced—or a little like the x and y axes that we know from mathematics. Because we supplied these concepts rather than gaining them from our experiences and upbringing, Kant called these the pure concepts, or pure categories. We supplied this framework of categories, and experience filled it.

Kant's approach set the stage for various modifications of the idea that we impose categories on our experience. Kant believed that all human beings had the same categories and that, although we could know what they were, we could have no meaningful experience "outside" of them. Thinkers in our century have modified this approach somewhat; our categories have often been seen as more or less closely related to our culture, history, or specific language. What, then, is the relationship between these paradigms through which we view and experience the world and our "selves"? To what extent can we step out of these paradigms, even as a thought experiment, to learn to avoid imposing our preexisting categories or frameworks on others and our world? On the one hand, the concepts and expectations that we bring to situations help us navigate events without reinventing the wheel at each step. However, on the other hand, the same paradigms that serve us well in many situations may also block us from recognizing new ideas and modifying ourselves to confront changed circumstances. In this third stage, we will look at these matters.

The two texts for this session assist us in exploring how we impose ourselves on our experience. Both Francis Bacon and Simone Weil examine this phenomenon. Bacon lists a number of sources of the confusion of our understanding. He calls these false opinions idols, referring to the idols to which people once prayed. He describes four different types of idols—those related to human nature, our nation or culture, our contacts and dealings with one another, and our systems of philosophy. In the second text, Weil does not look at the sources, but rather at how words that have no meaning affect our actions. In her view, these empty words cause us to struggle with one another and to fight terrible wars. Since the words about which we struggle represent nothing at all, she contends, we cannot compromise and settle our disagreements.

Worksheet 11

The unit introduction highlights the complexity of language, the difficulties we have in communicating with one another, and our tendency to impose ourselves on whatever we encounter. The texts by Bacon and Weil consider, in different ways, the power of thought and language to lead us astray. The worksheet asks us to rank the members of our group according to their ability to listen genuinely. This exercise is undertaken not so much for the purpose of ranking our group members but for the purpose of forcing us to determine some criteria for deciding whether someone is a good listener.

1. On a separate sheet of paper, please evaluate privately the listening skills of the members of the group, including you, by putting names or initials along a line like the one below. The scale ranges from 1(a poor listener) to 10 (an excellent listener).

      1 _____ 5 _____ 10

2. What criteria did you use to determine your highest ranking?

3. What criteria did you use to determine your lowest ranking?

4. Why did you give yourself the ranking you did?

5. After reading the texts, write an opening question for the discussion.

The New Organon
by Francis Bacon

False opinions, which I call idols, have now taken possession of the human understanding. They have taken such deep root in men's minds that truth can hardly find entrance. But even if truth does find an entrance, the false opinions or idols will meet and trouble us at the very creation of the sciences. This can only be avoided if men are warned in advance of the danger and can strengthen themselves as much as possible against the assaults.

There are four different types of false opinions or four idols that cloud all men's minds. To distinguish these I have given them names. They are first, the Idols of the Tribe; second, the Idols of the Cave; third, the Idols of the Marketplace; and fourth, the Idols of the Theater. To guard ourselves from these idols and false beliefs, we should form our ideas and axioms only by true reasoning from experience.

1. Idols of the Tribe are based in human nature itself, and hold in their grip all the tribe or race of men. These false opinions are founded in our commonest belief that our senses are a measure and good indicator of the truth about things. However, the human understanding and the senses are like a distorting mirror that changes and colors what we see by adding its own nature to it.

2. The Idols of the Cave are the false beliefs of each individual man. For everyone (besides errors common to human nature) has a cave or den of his own. Each person changes and colors the light of nature because of his own particular nature, his education, the books he reads, the authorities he believes, the differences between his sensations and those of others, and whether his mind is preoccupied or calm.

3. There are also Idols formed by the association of men with each other. These I call Idols of the Marketplace because that is where men associate with one another. And these Idols or false beliefs are contained in the very language we speak, for it is through speech that association occurs. Words are imposed on things according to the understanding of ordinary men. And poor or unfit choice of words wonderfully clouds the understanding. Nor do the definitions or explanations with which learned men try to guard and defend themselves set the matter right. Words throw all into confusion and lead men in numberless empty controversies and idle imaginings.

4. Last of all are the Idols that enter men's minds from the various systems of philosophy, through their false rules of reasoning and demonstration. These I call Idols of the Theater because in my judgment, all the systems of philosophy are but so many stage plays that represent worlds of their own creation in an unreal but scenic fashion.

Of all these, the most troublesome are the Idols of the Marketplace because of the ways words and names bring false beliefs into the understanding. Men believe that their reason governs words. But it is also true that words react on and affect the understanding. This is what has up to now made philosophy and science false and useless. Words are commonly made and applied according to the ability of the ordinary people. So, words classify things in the way most obvious to the ordinary understanding. Whenever a person whose understanding is more acute or who observes more carefully would change the classifications of things to agree better with the true divisions in nature, words themselves stand in the way and resist change. So it often happens that serious discussions by learned men often end in disputes about words and names. Following the wise practice of mathematicians, a discussion about words would be a better way to begin, and then by means of definitions we might reduce words to order. Yet even definitions cannot cure this evil when dealing with natural and material things. This is because definitions themselves consist of words and these words are linked with yet others.

The false beliefs imposed by words are of two kinds. The first sort of false beliefs result from the names of things that do not exist. For just as there are things that have not yet been named through a lack of observation, so also there are names that result from fantastic ideas and to which nothing in reality corresponds. The second type of false beliefs comes from words that do name things that exist but whose names are confused, not well defined, and derived from reality in a careless and hasty way. Examples of words that name nothing are "luck," "heat," and a "first mover of things." These fictions owe their origin to false theories. It is therefore easy to get rid of these Idols, because we need only reject the theories that give them birth. However, words that come from faulty and unskillful reasoning from experience cause false beliefs that are deeply rooted.

The Power of Words
by Simone Weil

The security we enjoy in our time is due to technology that gives us much control over nature. This security is more than cancelled by the danger of destruction we face because of conflicts between groups of men. The danger is great because of the power of destructive weapons supplied by technology. But weapons do not fire themselves, and it is dishonest to blame things for a situation in which all the responsibility is man's. All our worst struggles share a characteristic that may seem reassuring, but that is really the greatest danger: Our conflicts have no definite purpose or goal. All of history shows that it is especially such conflicts that are the most bitter. It may be that understanding this is one of the keys to all of history—it is certainly the key to our own times.

In a struggle that is about a well defined objective, each of the parties can decide if the risks do or do not outweigh the benefits. They can then decide whether it is worth fighting. Usually they find that they can come to a compromise which is more beneficial even than winning the battle. But when there is no well-defined stake, it isn't possible to compare alternatives, and therefore it isn't possible to compromise. In this situation, the only possible standard for the importance of a war is the number of sacrifices that have been made to fight it. The sacrifices that have already been made are always taken as reason for making yet more sacrifices. Thus there is never a reason to stop killing and dying, except that people's endurance for suffering has limits.

The most perfect example of this sort of war is known to every so-called educated person, but we read about it without understanding it. The Greeks and Trojans killed one another for ten years on account of Helen. No one except for Paris cared about her at all. Everyone wished that she had never been born. Helen was so insignificant compared to the size of the battle that no one really believed that the war was about her. But the real issue was never defined by anyone, because there never was a real issue. The importance of the war was measured by the number of people already killed and the number who were going to be killed. This made the war seem so important that no one questioned it. No one felt that the price of the war was too great, because all were in pursuit of something that did not exist and whose only value was the price paid for it. Nowadays people think that wars like this, which seem to have no real objective, are actually being fought because people are being manipulated by economic interests. The people in Homer's time blamed these wars on the gods. But there is no need to imagine gods or economic conspiracies to understand why human beings rush into disaster. Human nature is enough to explain this.

For a person who really sees what is going on today, there is nothing sadder than the unreal character of contemporary wars. They have even less reality than the war between the Greeks and Trojans. In that case, at least, there was a woman, and a very beautiful one. In our time, the role of Helen is played by words in capital letters, swollen with blood and tears. If we grab one of these words and squeeze it, we find that it is empty. Words that have real meanings are not murderous. But when empty words are given capital letters, then, with the smallest excuse, men will kill for the sake of these words. They will destroy and kill without knowing exactly what these words refer to, for the simple reason that they refer to nothing. In this situation, the only definition of success is to crush some other group of men that is fighting for the sake of a different, hostile word. It is a characteristic of empty words that each of them has another empty word that is its special enemy.

Clear thinking and precise analysis are very hard to do in our own modern age. We appear to be very sophisticated and to know about many things. Unlike the Greeks, we appear not to be superstitious. However, this shiny surface hides the real weakness of our thought. Superstition has entered our thought in a hidden way through the vocabulary of science. Our science is like a department store filled with clever tools for solving complex problems. Yet, we seem to have lost the power of thought when we turn to questions not covered by science. When we think about social and political questions, our talk becomes filled with the monsters of a new superstition and mythology. The words we use are abstract and absolute, meaningless words with capital letters. Examples of these words are: nation, security, capitalism, communism, fascism, order, authority, property, and democracy. We never say, "there is democracy to the extent that…" or "there is capitalism insofar as…" When we use such words, we have a hard time using phrases like "insofar as." Words like democracy and capitalism have an absolute reality for us, which is not influenced by the conditions of life. At the same time, we make these words mean whatever we want. Our lives are lived in the middle of changing conditions, in which things change in specific and limited ways. Yet we act, and expect others to act, by reference to absolute realities, as if we were doing science. In this age of technicians, the only wars we know how to fight are wars that are not about anything.

Discussion Evaluation Form

The items below are discussion dynamics that may or may not be present in your group. Decide to what extent you think that each dynamic was present in the discussion. Then decide whether you think the group needs to work to improve in this area.

	None Some Great deal	Need to Improve?
Dominance by some individuals	1 2 3 4 5 6 7 8 9 10	Yes ❏ No ❏
Cooperation	1 2 3 4 5 6 7 8 9 10	Yes ❏ No ❏
Silence	1 2 3 4 5 6 7 8 9 10	Yes ❏ No ❏
Interrupting	1 2 3 4 5 6 7 8 9 10	Yes ❏ No ❏
Respect	1 2 3 4 5 6 7 8 9 10	Yes ❏ No ❏
Balanced participation	1 2 3 4 5 6 7 8 9 10	Yes ❏ No ❏
Active listening	1 2 3 4 5 6 7 8 9 10	Yes ❏ No ❏
Lack of interest	1 2 3 4 5 6 7 8 9 10	Yes ❏ No ❏
Asking one other questions	1 2 3 4 5 6 7 8 9 10	Yes ❏ No ❏
Building on one other's contributions	1 2 3 4 5 6 7 8 9 10	Yes ❏ No ❏
Many people talking at once	1 2 3 4 5 6 7 8 9 10	Yes ❏ No ❏

Pick one of the dynamics that you think the group should work to improve, and explain why.

How would you rate this discussion on a scale of 1–10? _____

12

What We Share

Little is more frustrating than speaking and not being understood or than finding our thoughts misrepresented by people who are quite convinced they understood us. Many of us have been in situations in which we have supposedly been quoted or paraphrased and what is stated has no resemblance to what we remember having said. Toward the end of his life, the Emperor Augustus was so concerned with the possibility of being misrepresented that he is reported to have refused to speak and to have communicated only in writing. He was so aware that his words could affect millions of lives that he wished to protect himself from being misunderstood. Of course there is no guarantee that writing is any less difficult a form of communication. Some people, including Plato, hold that because writers, unlike speakers, are often not available to answer our questions, writing is the more problematic of the two ways of communicating.

Most of us are familiar with the children's game telephone, in which a message is passed by being whispered from one person to the next. By the time it has passed through a few people, the conveyed message typically bears almost no resemblance to the original one. Speaking involves a risk of misunderstanding and miscommunication. The possibility of miscommunication is a factor in all cases of speaking to others, but such a risk is especially a factor in a discussion. Why is it so troubling when we are not understood or when our words are misquoted? Perhaps it is because our words are not just an accidental characteristic of who we are and what we do. They give meaning to our actions and our relationships with others. It is an understatement to say that our words represent us. Rather, our words are, in many ways, our presence in the world. We don't just own our words as we might other forms of property. Our words are us. To violate our words through inattention, misunderstanding, or misquoting is in some measure to violate us. It therefore becomes imperative for us to genuinely listen and attempt to understand one another's words, even if we don't agree with them.

Philosophy, often described as a search for truths we can all share, has traditionally been considered a crucial aid in listening and understanding. This search for truth has sometimes focused, as in the writings of Plato, on uncovering what we bring *to* the world; or, as in the writings of Aristotle, on locating the ideas or concepts we all can gain from our experience *of* the world. For Plato, we all bring certain very general ideas into the world—ideas such as justice, beauty, equality, and the notions of "same" and "different." These last two ideas enable us to structure our experience in relation to the similarities and differences among things. Aristotle held that we share a common logic or way of thinking about the world. Logic for Aristotle is based on the most certain and fundamental truth about all things in the world, including our thoughts. This we call the Law of Non-Contradiction. It states in a current formulation that the same thing cannot both have and not have a specific characteristic at the same time and in the same way. An example is that the table in one's room cannot be both green and not green in the same exact place and time. However, the table could be green on the top and not green or brown on its legs or green one month and then painted brown sometime later. Aristotle also believed that beyond this basic logic, there were other truths we could all share but that arriving at these truths would take great effort.

During the period before the scientific revolution in the sixteenth and seventeenth centuries, when theological and Christian attitudes dominated the West, a different view came into prominence. Leading thinkers believed that people misunderstood one another because of our attitudes toward others and the world. The problem was our pride and self-will rather than our conflicting sets of assumptions or opinions. This thinking about pride is reflected in the biblical story of the tower of Babel. According to many interpretations of the story, pride led people to try to make a name for themselves and to try to rival God by erecting a tower that reached to heaven. For this early foray into technology, our reward was the confusion of tongues—the creation of multiple languages. Misunderstanding, then, is seen to be the direct result of overweening pride. In the New Testament account of this story, the confusion of languages at Babel was counteracted by the descent of the Holy Spirit on the apostles on Pentecost. This event allowed the apostles to communicate the gospel in all languages. It is interesting to note that the confusion of Babel was counteracted in a different way than one might have expected. We did not all suddenly return to a single original speech; the various languages continued to exist. Misunderstanding is overcome in this account not by having everyone speak the same language but by listening and speaking in a new spirit. Here, misunderstanding is a willful, uncharitable act, rather than the simple result of a language barrier or an inability to understand.

This unit features three texts that allow us to reflect on these issues. In the first text, Plato claims that some of the standards that we use to judge what we sense were actually present before birth or—as some modern thinkers claim—these standards are prewired into our brains. In the second text, Emilie du Chatelet claims that all human beings share a logic that expresses the inevitable workings of our minds. In agreement with Plato and Aristotle and also with much of modern science, she contends that we have a shared natural logic in our thinking that can act as a bridge to enable us to understand one another. In the third text, Ludwig Wittgenstein views with suspicion the supposed status of logic as an ultimate foundation. He does not see philosophy as the effort to find our shared opinions but rather as the effort to free us from certain obsessive desires and expectations. He does not advocate a religious solution of the type mentioned earlier in this introduction, although he is closer to that view than to the scientific one. Philosophy, for him, must change its approach and not model itself on science. Instead it should become similar to therapy. In Wittgenstein's work, it almost sounds as if philosophy is a therapy to free us from a neurosis that gets in our way of understanding others, the world, and ourselves. Such a view would make his approach closer to the sense that our attitudes rather than our beliefs stop us from understanding one another. For Wittgenstein, we are not open to hearing something new, and perhaps the therapy could open us up to what another person is thinking.

Worksheet 12

The introduction explores the question of why misunderstanding occurs among us. The texts by Plato, Chatelet, and Wittgenstein propose differing accounts of what we share and where the possibilities for genuine connection with one another lie. The worksheet names three means—religion, philosophy, and science—by which people have often attempted to arrive at some sort of truth we would all share, and asks to which of them we ourselves would turn to answer certain questions.

1. The questions listed below are similar to ones that have absorbed people for many centuries. Some people have felt that they found answers—either yes or no—whereas others have contended that no answer could be found. Those who found yes or no answers used various approaches or methods to reach their conclusions; some used a religious approach, some a philosophical approach, and some a scientific approach. For each question below, decide which discipline—religion, philosophy, or science—would be most likely to supply a definite yes or no answer for you.

	Religion	Philosophy	Science
a) Does the universe end?	❏	❏	❏
b) Is there a God?	❏	❏	❏
c) Do humans cause global warming?	❏	❏	❏
d) Is there life after death?	❏	❏	❏
e) Will there always be wars?	❏	❏	❏
f) Can a person live forever?	❏	❏	❏
g) Will all human action someday be explained by science?	❏	❏	❏
h) Will science eventually cure all diseases?	❏	❏	❏
i) Can technology improve the world?	❏	❏	❏

2. In question 1, you decided what questions could be best answered by religion, philosophy, and science. Briefly explain your reasons for choosing religion, philosophy, or science for particular questions.

   a) When I selected religion, it was because:

   b) When I selected philosophy, it was because:

   c) When I selected science, it was because:

3. Write a question you would like to use to open the discussion.

The Phaedo
by Plato

Socrates: Before we began to see and hear and use our other senses, we must somewhere have acquired the knowledge that there is such a thing as perfect equality. If not, then how could we ever have realized, by using it as a standard for comparison, that everything we see that appears equal is not quite equal but only an imperfect image of equality. We know that two sticks we call equal are only approximately equal and not truly equal. So it seems this knowledge came with us into the world. And what we have claimed of equality is equally true of all other qualities we believe can be perfect—such as beauty, goodness, uprightness, and holiness.

Philosophical Grammar
by Emilie du Chatelet

Grammar is the system of rules by means of which we all describe the way in which languages represent what is going on in our minds. The different languages that different societies speak have their origins in human needs and are very different from one another. However, all languages are based on the natural logic that all human beings have in their minds. Although we don't always know the rules of grammar when we speak, we are always expressing the workings of our minds and thus using the natural logic that all human beings have. This is why the rules of grammar are nearly the same in all languages. You cannot understand language unless you understand logic.

Whenever we experience something in the world, we do one of three things to it. We first perceive it, then we make judgments about it, and finally, we try to learn more about it. From the point of view of language, judging is our most important activity. This is because when we speak, we almost always find ourselves making judgments. We rarely ever simply want to express our perceptions of something. In fact, whenever we try to express a simple perception, we find ourselves making a judgment. For example, suppose I am talking to other people and say, "I see a man." I am, in this case, judging that the object that I perceive has the collection of characteristics to which I am in the habit of giving the name, "man." Therefore, what human beings produce by speaking is a collection of words that stand for a judgment of the mind. We rarely describe an experience by saying, "I see a patch six feet high and about two feet wide that is green on top and blue on the bottom." Instead, we say, "I see a man six feet tall wearing a green shirt and blue pants."

Since every collection of words expresses a judgment of the mind, each of these collections always contains three kinds of words. First, there is the subject, what we are talking about. Second is the attribute, what we are saying about the subject. Third, there are the words that join the subject to the attribute, or separate the subject from the attribute. For example, "This man is wearing a green jacket," or "This man is not wearing a green jacket." In every judgment we make, in no matter which language, we say that something either does or does not have certain attributes.

It is true that we don't always say these kinds of words when we speak. However, they are always contained in what we say, since what we say is based on natural logic, and these kinds of words express natural logic. Therefore, the most natural and general division of words is into those that stand for the things we perceive (the subject, "man," and the attributes "green shirt," "blue coat"), and those that stand for our judgments about these perceptions ("wearing," "not wearing"). So, though all languages may differ from one another in other ways, all must have these three kinds of words. For these words come from the natural logic that all minds use.

Philosophical Investigations
by Ludwig Wittgenstein

I

These considerations bring us up to the philosophical problem: In what sense is logic something sublime?

Thinkers imagined that logic was the deepest foundation of our thought. Logic seemed to have a universal significance. Logic lay, it seemed, at the bottom of all the sciences. For doesn't logical investigation seem to explore the nature of all things? It seeks to see to the bottom of things and is not meant to concern itself whether what actually happens is this or that. It takes its rise, neither from an interest in the facts of nature nor from a need to grasp how something causes something else, but from an urge to understand the basis, or essence, of everything we experience. Not, however, as if to this end we had to hunt out new facts. It is, we all imagine, the essence of a logical investigation that we do not seek to learn anything new by it. We want to understand something that is already in plain view. For this is what we seem in some sense not to understand.

Augustine says in the *Confessions*, "What is time? If no one asks me, I know. If someone asks me to explain, I no longer know." This could not be said about a question of natural science ("What is the specific gravity of hydrogen?" for instance). Something that we know when no one asks us but no longer know when we are supposed to give an account of it, is something that we need to remind ourselves of. (And it is obviously something of which for some reason it is difficult to remind oneself.)

And this applies to our questions about logic.

II

Philosophers want to say that there can't be any vagueness in logic. But isn't this just an idea that now absorbs us? We are convinced that the ideal "must" be found in reality. Meanwhile we do not as yet see how it occurs there, nor do we understand the nature of this "must." We think it must be in reality, for we think we already see it there.

III

What is common to all games? Don't say "There must be something in common or they would not be called games." But look and see whether there is anything in common to them. For if you look, you will not see anything in common but similarities, relationships, and a whole series of them at that. I repeat: Don't think, but look!

IV

It is not our aim to refine or complete the system of rules for the use of our words in unheard-of ways.

For the clarity that we are aiming at is indeed complete clarity. But this simply means that the philosophical problems should completely disappear.

The real discovery is the one that makes me capable of stopping doing philosophy when I want to. The one that gives philosophy peace, so that it is no longer tormented by questions that bring itself in question. Instead, we now demonstrate a method, by examples, and the series of examples can be broken off. Problems are solved (difficulties eliminated), not a *single* problem.

There is not *a* philosophical method, though there are indeed methods, like different therapies.

V

We must do away with all explanation, and description alone must take its place. And this description, as in II, gets its importance, that is to say its purpose, from the philosophical problems—in that instance about philosophers' claims about logic. These are, of course, not scientific and factual problems. They are solved, rather, by looking into the workings of our language and doing so in such a way as to make us recognize how language works: in spite of our urge to misunderstand the workings of language. The problems that have haunted philosophers are solved, not by giving new information, but by arranging what we have always known. Our philosophical investigations are a battle against the bewitchment of our intelligence by means of language.

VI

A picture held us captive. And we could not get outside it for it lay in our language and language seemed to repeat it to us inexorably.

VII

The results of philosophy are the uncovering of one or another piece of plain nonsense and the bumps that the understanding has got by running its head up against the limits of language.

Discussion Evaluation Form

The items below are discussion dynamics that may or may not be present in your group. Decide to what extent you think that each dynamic was present in the discussion. Then decide whether you think the group needs to work to improve in this area.

	None Some Great deal	Need to Improve?
Dominance by some individuals	1 2 3 4 5 6 7 8 9 10	Yes ❏ No ❏
Cooperation	1 2 3 4 5 6 7 8 9 10	Yes ❏ No ❏
Silence	1 2 3 4 5 6 7 8 9 10	Yes ❏ No ❏
Interrupting	1 2 3 4 5 6 7 8 9 10	Yes ❏ No ❏
Respect	1 2 3 4 5 6 7 8 9 10	Yes ❏ No ❏
Balanced participation	1 2 3 4 5 6 7 8 9 10	Yes ❏ No ❏
Active listening	1 2 3 4 5 6 7 8 9 10	Yes ❏ No ❏
Lack of interest	1 2 3 4 5 6 7 8 9 10	Yes ❏ No ❏
Asking one other questions	1 2 3 4 5 6 7 8 9 10	Yes ❏ No ❏
Building on one other's contributions	1 2 3 4 5 6 7 8 9 10	Yes ❏ No ❏
Many people talking at once	1 2 3 4 5 6 7 8 9 10	Yes ❏ No ❏

Pick one of the dynamics that you think the group should work to improve, and explain why.

How would you rate this discussion on a scale of 1–10? _____

13

Listening for Differences

For this meeting, we will consider our first text from a non-Western culture—a reading from ancient China. We will discuss a text by Mencius, a political thinker who traveled from court to court, and compare it with a work by President Woodrow Wilson of the United States. Thus far, the *Mapping the Future* program has focused on Western texts because these texts contain the sources of the concepts and categories that have become our presuppositions and that in Touchstones we wish to investigate. These categories form the foundation of most Western societies, and through the influence of Western ideas and political systems, much of the world. On a more personal level, they are also the presuppositions that have emerged as issues to be overcome in establishing a discussion group. Thus, we have looked at these Western texts as tools to enable us to discern many invisible features of our own thinking, not as works that are more important or significant than texts from other cultures. However, texts from foreign cultures are also invaluable tools in our effort to see ourselves more clearly. They frequently connect us with ideas that differ sharply from our own ways of understanding the world. Considering such different ideas can be crucial for our investigation for two reasons. First, it highlights our own views by way of contrast; second, it opens up new areas of exploration by revealing new possibilities. We are so accustomed to some of our own opinions that we imagine that any modification or change is impossible until we recognize that entire civilizations, some of which have lasted thousands of years, viewed the world quite differently. Texts from distant cultures reveal to us that change in our fundamental beliefs is possible. They present alternative views that might otherwise seem impossible, given our proximity to our culture's attitudes.

Reading texts from another culture can raise some familiar but also unique difficulties. Some difficulties are of course present in reading even texts from an earlier period of our culture. When we examine a text from the seventeenth century or from ancient Greece, some of the issues and concerns are familiar and some are at odds with our current habits or attitudes. With texts from our own tradition, we are like archeologists. As archeologists, we are familiar with certain aspects of the terrain we are investigating because we can discern similarities with our own situations. Often we are examining the very ancestors of our ideas. We therefore see these texts as earlier versions of ourselves. This gives us a place to start reading them and trying to articulate the perspective of the writer—which in many ways differs from our own. In reading such texts, we must then restrain ourselves from dismissing differences as quaint ideas that we have outgrown or that we now realize are false. Instead, we should begin to seek the unity of the aspects that we recognize and still maintain with those that seem strange or outdated.

The difficulties with texts from a culture that is foreign to our own are of a different sort. With such texts, we are less like archeologists than we are like explorers. In dealing with a text from another culture, we must not assume that our current ways of thinking are an outgrowth of any similar ones reflected in the foreign text. It is true that over the recorded past there have been many contacts between the West and other cultures that have given us such influential tools as our alphabet and number system. However, we must take care that the historical fact of contact and exchange between diverse cultures is not used as a way to play down genuine differences through an emphasis on superficial similarities.

In fact, the artifacts, texts, and concepts that were incorporated into our own culture were able to flourish there because a framework already existed that they were somehow able to fill. For example, in the nineteenth century, many texts from India were brought into the West and became very popular, and many Buddhist and Zen ideas became current. However, the intellectual movements of the late eighteenth and early nineteenth centuries in Germany and France prepared the way for this influx by raising philosophical and religious issues to which these Eastern ideas seemed to respond. In other words, the versions of Eastern thought that survived were co-opted and adapted to meet particular predetermined Western needs. They were versions that (1) fit into a set of issues and beliefs we already had and (2) had been stripped from the surroundings in which they had their original meaning. Thus the fact that the language and concepts of a text from a distant culture may seem somewhat familiar to us should not lead us to assume that the ideas we are encountering are actually contiguous with our own.

When faced with a text from a foreign culture, we often tend toward one of two typical reactions. We either assume too much similarity between our own ideas and those in the text, or we tend to focus too exclusively on the differences. We might read the texts through our own presuppositions and assimilate them too easily to our own established perspective, or we might be shocked by their "foreignness" and think that they have no connection with anything we believe. In both instances, such texts cease being useful tools. When we overemphasize the similarities, we discount the differences in our languages and the influences of thousands of years of history and different ideas of law, government, religion, science, and the value of life. We imagine that the text is a part of our own culture or that it reflects an underlying human nature with which we are familiar. But this is not an assumption we should allow ourselves in Touchstones. Conversely, when we focus too much on the differences, it may seem that we have no possible point of contact with what we are reading.

Our task in reading a text from a distant culture is to attempt, with the help of the translator, to imagine another world. The accomplished translator stands in both the world of the text and the world of the reader, creating a bridge to allow the reader access to the text. However, the task of crossing that bridge is still ours. It requires both an awareness of the ways in which our own cultural presuppositions shape our thoughts and a willingness to experiment with different ways of seeing the world. Thus the attempt to enter another world—whether or not we believe it is possible—is a very important activity as we seek to examine our own perspectives. We will undertake this activity through the text from Mencius by trying to examine the parts that seem to make sense in a Western context and those that strike us as far removed and alien. Comparing it with the passage by Wilson will assist us in this task.

Mencius gives a central place in his work to what he calls benevolence. This concept plays a role that has an importance that we normally do not give it. For us, a person who is not benevolent is still a human being. That person might not be someone we admire or someone we wish to know but still that person is fully human. For Mencius, however, that trait is something that plays a deeper role in how he understands human beings and their role in the world. In the excerpt from Wilson, he looks at benevolence in an unusual but still recognizable way. For him, it is a higher form of entrepreneurial activity and not just an additional trait in everyone's life. Wilson claims that for certain people, it is the culmination of activities that we don't normally consider continuous with benevolence. Many people view business and benevolence as coming from two different sources, but Wilson agues that benevolence is a more complex form of the spirit that animates the investor or industrialist.

Worksheet 13

The unit's introduction addresses ways in which we approach difference, particularly the types of difference that often confront us across cultural boundaries. In the texts by Mencius and Woodrow Wilson—giving us Eastern and Western analyses of ways in which people should be involved with the world—we see an example of this type of difference. The worksheet asks us, as inhabitants of the West, to examine more closely our reaction to the Mencius text by comparing his ideas with our basic comprehension of what it means to be fully human.

1. As you read each one of the four sections in the passage from Mencius, evaluate how close each section is to Western ideas. Use a scale of 1 to 10, with 1 being the farthest and 10 being the closest.

    Section I _____   Section II _____   `

    Section III _____   Section IV _____

2. Consider the part of Section II in which Mencius describes four aspects that characterize what it is to be human. Mencius claims these four characteristics give rise to the following four principles: benevolence, righteousness, propriety, and knowledge. Do you consider all four of these characteristics essential to what it means to be human? Why or why not?

3. Which characteristic do you consider to be most important in defining a human being? Is there another you would propose?

4. Imagine that you are a translator. Do the translations of the four characteristics seem appropriate, or would you use different English words to capture what is meant?

5. After reading the texts, write an opening question for the discussion.

The Seven Books
by Mencius

I

Mencius went to see King Hwuy of Leang. "Honored sir," the King said to Mencius. "Since you have not considered it too far to travel here, though it is a distance of over a thousand miles, may I presume to ask if you have advice that can profit my kingdom?"

Mencius replied, "Why must Your Majesty use that word *profit*? I do indeed have advice, but it is always about righteousness and benevolence. If Your Majesty says, 'What can profit my kingdom?' the generals and high officials will say, 'What can profit our families?' The lower officials and the common people will ask, 'How can we profit ourselves?' Everyone will try to seize this profit, and the kingdom will be threatened. If righteousness is put last and profit first, then no one will be satisfied without seizing everything. There has never been a man trained to righteousness who didn't think first of his sovereign. Let Your Majesty say, 'Benevolence and righteousness shall be our only themes.' Why must you use that word *profit*?"

II

Mencius said, "Men's minds cannot bear to see the sufferings of others. My meaning can be illustrated by this example. Even in these days, if we suddenly see a child about to fall into a well, we all experience a feeling of alarm and distress. We do not feel this way because we want the favor of the child's parents or the praise of our friends and neighbors. Nor do we feel this way because we are afraid of getting a reputation for callousness. We simply feel distressed when we see a child about to be injured.

"From this example, we can recognize that without a feeling for the misery and suffering of another, we would not be human. Nor would we be human if we didn't feel shame for our own lack of goodness, and anger and distaste at its absence in others. No less important to what we are is our feeling of modesty. In modesty, we separate ourselves from our own concerns and desires, and recognize the concerns and desires in others. The last feeling that makes us human is our approval of what is good and our disapproval of what isn't. The feeling for another's misery is the principle of benevolence. The feeling of shame and anger is the principle of righteousness. The feeling of modesty is the principle of propriety or of what is one's own. The feeling of approval and disapproval is the principle of knowledge."

III

Mencius said, "If someone loves others, and others do not love him in return, let him turn inward and examine his own benevolence. If someone tries to rule others and his rule is unsuccessful, let him turn inward and examine his own wisdom. If he treats others politely and they do not return his politeness, let him turn inward and examine his own feeling of respect. When, by our efforts, we do not achieve what we desire, we must turn inward and examine ourselves in what we do. When someone really acts correctly, the whole empire turns to him with recognition and submission."

IV

Mencius said, "What distinguishes a superior man from others is what he holds in his heart; namely, benevolence and propriety. The benevolent man loves others. The man of propriety shows others respect. He who loves others is loved by them. He who respects others is always respected by them.

"What if we meet a man who treats us in a perverse and unreasonable way? In such a situation, the superior man will first turn around upon himself. He will say to himself, 'I must have been lacking in benevolence; I must have been lacking in propriety. How did this happen in me?' He examines himself and is especially benevolent. He turns around on himself and is especially observant of propriety. However, what if the other's perversity and unreasonableness remain the same? The superior man will again turn around on himself and say, 'I must have been failing to do my utmost.' He again turns on himself and makes even greater exertions. However, the perversity and unreasonableness may well continue. If they do, the superior man now says, 'This man is utterly lost. Since he acts in this way, he is no different from an animal, and why should I struggle with an animal?'"

When a Man Comes to Himself
by Woodrow Wilson

It is a mistake to suppose that the great captains of industry, the great organizers and directors of manufacturing, commerce, and banking, are engrossed in a vulgar pursuit of wealth. Too often they allow the vulgarity of wealth to show itself in the idleness and display of their wives and children, who devote themselves to expense, regardless of pleasure. However, we ought not misunderstand even that nor condemn it unjustly. The masters of industry are often too busy with their own sober and important calling to have time to spare thought enough to govern their own households. A king may be too faithful a statesman to be a watchful father. These men are not fascinated by the glitter of gold; the appetite for power has got hold of them. They love to use their abilities on a great scale. They are organizing and overseeing a great part of the life of the world. No wonder they are in love with their work. Business is more interesting than pleasure, and once the mind has been caught by its excitement, there's no disengaging it. The world has reason to be grateful for this fact.

It was this fascination that had got hold of a man whom the world was afterward to know, not as a prince among merchants—for the world forgets merchant princes—but as a prince among benefactors. The first time he was asked to give money for a worthy object, he declined. Why should he give? What project would be helped? What increase of efficiency would the money buy? What return would it bring in? Was good money simply to be given away, like water poured on barren soil, to be sucked up and yield nothing? It was not until men who understood benevolence explained to him that it is a kind of investment that his mind turned to it for satisfaction. They explained it as something very systematic and practical. He began to see that investment in others' education was really profitable, that money devoted to it would yield returns to which there was no end, and that the increase was perpetual. The result would be an invisible but intensely real spiritual interest beyond reckoning, because compounded in an unknown ratio from age to age. Henceforward, benevolence was as interesting to him as business. Indeed, it was a sort of refined business in which money moved new forces in an exchange that no man could bind or limit.

This man had come to himself—to the full realization of his powers, the true and clear perception of what it was his mind demanded for its satisfaction. But, there is a negative side also. Men come to themselves by discovering their limitations, no less than by discovering their deeper gifts and the mastery that will make them happy. It is the discovery of what they cannot do, and ought not to attempt, that transforms reformers into statesmen. No statesman dreams of doing whatever he pleases. He knows that it does not follow that because a point of morals or of policy is obvious to him, it will be obvious to the nation or even to his own friends. It is the strength of a democratic society that there are so many minds to be consulted and brought to agreement. Social reform is a matter of cooperation. If it is new, it requires a great deal of persuading to bring the majority to believe in it and support it. Without their agreement and support, it is impossible.

Often, the most immediate and drastic means of bringing men to themselves is to elect them to legislative or executive office. That will reduce overconfident persons to their simplest. It is not that such men lose courage when they find themselves charged with the actual direction of the affairs concerning which they have held and uttered such strong, unhesitating, and drastic opinions. They have only learned discretion. For the first time, they see in its entirety what it was that they were attempting. They are, at last, at close quarters with the world. Men of every interest and type crowd about them; new impressions strike them. In the midst of affairs, the former special objects of their zeal fall into new environments, a better and truer perspective. Things no longer seem so susceptible to separate and radical change. The real nature of the complex stuff of life they were seeking to work in is revealed to them—its intricate and delicate fiber, and the subtle, secret interrelationship of its parts. They work carefully, lest they should damage more than they fix. Moral enthusiasm is not, uninstructed and of itself, a suitable guide to practical and lasting reformation. And if the reform sought is the reformation of others as well as of himself, the reformer should look to it that he knows the true relation of his will to the wills of those he would change and guide. When he has discovered that relation, he has come to himself. Then he has discovered his real use and his part in planning for the world of men. He has come to the full command and satisfying use of his powers. Otherwise, he is doomed to live forever in a fool's paradise. He can be said to have come to himself only on the supposition that he is a fool.

Discussion Evaluation Form

The items below are discussion dynamics that may or may not be present in your group. Decide to what extent you think that each dynamic was present in the discussion. Then decide whether you think the group needs to work to improve in this area.

	None Some Great deal	Need to Improve?
Dominance by some individuals	1 2 3 4 5 6 7 8 9 10	Yes ❑ No ❑
Cooperation	1 2 3 4 5 6 7 8 9 10	Yes ❑ No ❑
Silence	1 2 3 4 5 6 7 8 9 10	Yes ❑ No ❑
Interrupting	1 2 3 4 5 6 7 8 9 10	Yes ❑ No ❑
Respect	1 2 3 4 5 6 7 8 9 10	Yes ❑ No ❑
Balanced participation	1 2 3 4 5 6 7 8 9 10	Yes ❑ No ❑
Active listening	1 2 3 4 5 6 7 8 9 10	Yes ❑ No ❑
Lack of interest	1 2 3 4 5 6 7 8 9 10	Yes ❑ No ❑
Asking one other questions	1 2 3 4 5 6 7 8 9 10	Yes ❑ No ❑
Building on one other's contributions	1 2 3 4 5 6 7 8 9 10	Yes ❑ No ❑
Many people talking at once	1 2 3 4 5 6 7 8 9 10	Yes ❑ No ❑

Pick one of the dynamics that you think the group should work to improve, and explain why.

How would you rate this discussion on a scale of 1–10? _____

14

Understanding Others

When we confront a belief from a foreign culture that doesn't immediately make sense or that even seems absurd, we have some readily available options for dealing with the difficulty. We can attribute the difficulty to the extreme difference between our paradigm or language and the other culture, or hypothesize that the culture's ideas were poorly translated. However, these options are not available when we face this difficulty with someone from our own culture or environment—for example, with another participant in the discussion group.

In this context, when we hear something that seems absurd or very much at odds with what we believe, the options for dealing with it are more circumscribed and can require very difficult decisions. When we share a culture, we naturally assume that we agree on fundamental beliefs. Therefore, when we cannot give a plausible account of the genesis of the difference between us and others from our own culture, we turn to external and more extreme factors to explain the disconnect. These factors often allow us not to take those ideas seriously or discount them altogether. For example, if the speaker has been ill, we might claim that the person is delirious or has said something because he or she is under the influence of some medication. We may wonder whether a person is drunk. These are ways that we may seek to give a physiological account of what was said and thus not take it seriously as an idea. Another route is to seek to dismiss an idea by saying that the person must be somehow psychologically unstable or must have spoken either jokingly or under the influence of extreme emotions—that is, "in the heat of the moment." In our discussion sessions, however, we must resist turning to these sorts of options—or any other strategies in which we totally discount another person's statements.

To explore the fundamental beliefs that we all share and to investigate new possibilities, we will all need to say some things that sound strange, illogical, or even bizarre. Such expression is necessary when we are exploring new territory. When we speak in such ways, we must be careful to keep in mind our responsibility to the group. We mustn't just say things to provoke a response. Rather we must be willing to share ideas even when we ourselves don't quite understand what we're saying and when we are struggling to explore unknown terrain. We are therefore asking others to assist us and not to dismiss what we are trying to articulate. We must also show this same restraint with respect to others. We too often ask for an explanation of something someone says before that person is able to express the thought in greater detail. To resist the temptation to do this will require that we trust that the speaker is making a good-faith effort to explore his or her idea. At this stage of the process, we must reorient ourselves toward our words. We must learn to surrender our ownership of what is often most precious to us. This reorientation does not mean that we should be indifferent to what we say, but that we should not think that we must ensure that our words are correctly understood. This process involves striking a difficult balance between our sense of ourselves and our responsibility to the group. What is the proper attitude when participating in an exploratory discussion?

The Touchstones Discussion session is best viewed as a period that is bracketed off from the rest of one's life. In a sense, the participants must leave themselves in the hall when they enter the room where the discussion is to be held. The reason for this is that the discussion environment is a place for exploration and experimentation. The participants need to be freed from their commitments to beliefs, and even from themselves, in order to try on different thoughts and ideas. We are not experimenting on external objects but on our thoughts, desires, and goals. We are trying on new perspectives and ideas to see how they fit and whether we should experiment further. In other words, we are trying on new selves. The discussion itself is best conceived as a form of play. This playtime is extremely serious yet can only occur if one is playful.

The approach to play that we need for a discussion is like the approach to play we took as children. Child's play is extremely serious for children. Through it, they try on new personas. In the process of discussion, we do something very similar. We can become truly serious about the very possibilities that we otherwise dismiss in our regular lives. Discussion is therefore a period of freedom. These thoughts that we will pursue together are an uncharted terrain. Sometimes we will sound illogical or uncertain. If the participants continue to speak with the certainty that they had in the first stage, then they are not truly experimenting. We as listeners need to restrain our desire to require that others "make sense." We as speakers must understand that we can trust the others not to attack us when we are probing a new idea; we are simply the point person for the group at that moment. At this stage, the discussions should be characterized by the participants relying on one another to examine an idea or issue—as if first one speaker gets a foothold, then the others move on ahead of the footing that has been secured. In the early stages of the program, we felt obligated as participants to ask people to explain themselves and justify what they said. Now the situation is reversed. Each of us should feel the responsibility to make sense of what the speaker has stated. The responsibility belongs as much to us as it does to the person who spoke. The questions we must ask ourselves are: What is blocking me from understanding and agreeing with what has been said? What do I need to surrender and deny about my beliefs to be able to consider that what I am hearing is true? How do I need the discussion leader to assist in this effort? How can I share that responsibility and help?

This attitude is radically different from the attitude we normally adopt when we discuss topics with others. We need to be willing to trust that we are exploring a new realm together and that each of us has a stake in developing new ideas. In the previous unit, we practiced suspending our usual beliefs in order to imagine alien possibilities in another culture. In this unit, we are adopting this attitude toward our culture and ourselves. In the session in which we considered what we share, we were imitating archeologists; in the session in which we examined another culture, we became explorers. In this session, we become more like poets. Just as poets use image and metaphor to bring out new concepts and visions of the world and of our roles in it, so do we extend concepts in a metaphorical way. Just as artists help us see the world in new ways and notice new things and give an increased importance to what was previously less important, so do we help one another see the world in new ways. The philosopher Friedrich Nietzsche once said that concepts were dead metaphors. In these discussions, we are turning concepts that have lost their vitality into new metaphors.

Both authors of the texts for this session are attempting to articulate what for their times were radical new ideas about fundamental concepts of our culture—the role of women and the description of the key professions and subject areas that we pursue. Jenny d'Hericourt critiques the understanding and practice of science, law, medicine, war, and education. She claims that, because these areas have only involved the talents and perspectives that men are able to bring to them, they have had a one-sided character. She proposes a fundamental rethinking of these subjects to enable them to display the gifts that women can contribute. She not only recommends this rethinking to enable these gifts to find a use but also contends that the subjects themselves are defective without the gifts of women. For example, she claims that science and philosophy have been very abstract and that they need to incorporate again the connection with the concrete that women—with their more intimate involvement in tending to the physical details of everyday life—could bring. This is an opinion that has been stated repeatedly over the last few years about modern philosophy and the mathematical science that holds sway in physics. Virginia Woolf, too, claims that women's values and talents are different from men's. Women's works are therefore misunderstood when they are judged by values that are not adequate to them—values based on the attitude and talents of men. Woolf implies that many cultural and social preconditions are necessary for the creation of great works and that these have never been available to women. She predicts that a new form of writing will emerge once women are able to have the same creative resources that men have had. Both authors, by envisioning a new organization of society, the emergence of new attitudes, and the fashioning of new concepts, are modeling the approach of the poet that we must undertake in our own explorations.

Worksheet 14

The unit's introduction presents the familiar question of difference, but this time, of difference as it confronts us not from another culture but from someone who shares our own cultural background. In the texts by Woolf and Hericourt, we have examples of women speaking out about their experiences in ways that deeply challenged the assumptions of their audiences. The worksheet asks us to rank a number of statements in order of believability and then to consider the criteria by which we arrived at our ranking.

1. Below are listed ten statements that many people would consider absurd or false or questionable. Rank these statements from 1 to 10, with 1 being the least absurd, false, or questionable and 10 being the most absurd, false, or questionable.

   _____ a) The square has three sides.

   _____ b) The table is both green and yellow everywhere.

   _____ c) We will not have winter this year.

   _____ d) $2 + 3 = 7$

   _____ e) He can read another person's mind.

   _____ f) I experienced the injury in his left arm when he was hit.

   _____ g) He is neither happy nor unhappy.

   _____ h) The sun stood still for three hours.

   _____ i) Time moved backward.

   _____ j) He can communicate with the dead.

2. Choose the statements you ranked 1, 5, and 10 and, in the spaces below, explain why you ranked them as you did—why you thought that these three statements were respectively least questionable, somewhere in between, and most absurd. A way to explain your ranking might be to state why you think each statement might sometimes be true or could possibly be true or could never under any circumstances be true.

   Statement Ranked 1:

   Statement Ranked 5:

   Statement Ranked 10:

3. List a statement, either from above or your own experience, that a number of people you
know believe but that you find absurd or very difficult to believe.

4. Write an opening question for the discussion.

A Woman's Philosophy of Woman
by Jenny d'Hericourt

You, gentlemen, describe woman in the following ways. She is more impressionable than man, since her nerves are more fully developed. Since she is weaker, she must attain what she wants by cleverness and strategy. Her weakness forces her to be careful. Her destiny as mother makes her terrified of destruction and war. Her more delicate constitution makes her fear and avoid competition and contention. She loves concrete things. She is, therefore, always inclined to transform thoughts into facts, to embody them in a fixed form. Instead of a sustained process of thought, she reasons by intuition or by a quick perception of a general relation. Woman is a better observer than man, and therefore more insightful. She attends to what surrounds her, and is, consequently, a better judge of the moral and intellectual value of those people she knows. She has a greater sense of beauty and a greater love of goodness. She is more orderly and economical, and looks after administrative details, though with a carefulness that is often childish. She is gentler and more patient than man. She loves what is weak; she protects what suffers. This is woman as you men paint her.

On this basis, you conclude the following. The vocation of woman is love, maternity, and the household. She is too impressionable, too gentle, to be a judge or lawmaker. She is too flighty to pursue science, and her kind of intelligence makes her unable to understand theories. She is too interested in particular things to be serious about general ideas. This excludes her from all professions that require serious study. Her place is therefore at the fireside to make man better, to help him, to care for him, to enable him to receive the joys of fatherhood. Her role is to fill the place of a good housewife.

Now gentlemen, I agree with all your observations about how women differ from men, but on this same basis, I reach entirely opposite conclusions.

1. Woman would correct the exaggerated tendency of man for abstract theories, and she would demonstrate the falsity of theories based on ideas that are supposedly prior to all experience. She would carry into philosophy and science her subtleness of observation and her love of concrete things. Vague metaphysics would disappear. All would recognize that a hypothesis is merely the starting place for further questioning. We would see that truth is always intelligible in its nature, however unknown it may be. We shall avoid making simple generalities into binding laws of nature. Thus, we will finally have a true philosophy and science because they will carry the imprint of both sexes.

2. By her quick intuition and acuteness of observation, woman alone can discover the cures for psychological diseases. Her dexterity will make her valuable in all delicate surgical operations. She should take the lead in treating diseases of women and children because she alone is capable of fully comprehending them. In addition, she has a special place in hospitals for the management of the entire establishment.

3. The presence of woman in judicial functions as juror and judge will be a guarantee of true human justice to all. Woman alone, through her gentleness, her mercy, her feelings of sympathy, and her subtleness of observation, can understand that society has its share of guilt in every crime that a criminal commits. So, society should be organized to prevent wrong rather than to punish it. This point of view, which is especially feminine, will transform the penitentiary system. Conscious of its own share of guilt, society will then repair in penitentiaries the fault of its carelessness. Society will be firm, yet kind and moralizing. In prisons, it will give the education that it should have given outside. Society will prepare halfway houses for freed convicts so that the hatred and horror, often shown them by men worse than themselves, will not drive these former prisoners into a second offense.

4. Under the direct influence of woman as lawmaker, we shall have a reconstruction of all laws. First and foremost, we will have measures to prevent crime. Compulsory education will play a large role. Then, the form of lawsuits will be simplified, the civil code recast, and all laws disadvantaging illegitimate children and enforcing the inequality of the sexes will be banished. Laws concerning morality will be more severe, but the criminal laws will be more rational and fair.

So, gentlemen, while accepting your data about woman, I come to different conclusions. In what I write, you can behold woman placed everywhere by the side of man, except in the hard labor from which machinery will soon release you, and in the military establishment, which probably will someday disappear.

Until now, institutions, laws, sciences, and philosophy have chiefly displayed the masculine imprint. All these things are, therefore, only half human. To become truly human, woman must be part of all these activities. She must be trained and cultivated like you. Don't fear that she will become like you. The rose and the carnation growing in the same soil, under the same sky, cared for by the same gardener, nonetheless remain rose and carnation. And they are each more beautiful as they are better cultivated. If as you claim, and I agree with, man and woman differ, a similar education will only make them differ more. Each of us will employ that education in the development of what is peculiar to our individual selves.

For the interests of all things and all people, it is necessary that woman should enter all of the professions. She must have her function in all of life's functions. For woman too, the general interest of humanity comes first, then comes that of the family that cannot go before it.

Women and Fiction
by Virginia Woolf

It is probable that both in life and in art, the values of a woman are not the values of a man. Thus, when a woman comes to write a novel, she will find that she is perpetually wishing to alter the established values—to make serious what appears insignificant to a man, and trivial what is to him important. And for that, of course, she will be criticized; for the critic of the opposite sex will be genuinely puzzled and surprised by an attempt to alter the current scale of values, and will sense in it not merely a difference of view, but a view that is weak, or trivial, or sentimental, because it differs from his own.

But here, too, women are coming to be more independent of opinion. They are beginning to respect their own sense of values. They are less interested, it would seem, in themselves; on the other hand, they are more interested in other women. In the early nineteenth century, women's novels were largely autobiographical. One of the motives that led them to write was the desire to expose their own suffering to plead their cause. Now that this desire is no longer urgent, women are beginning to explore their own sex, to write of women as women have never been written of before; for of course, until very lately, women in literature were the creation of men.

Here again there are difficulties to overcome, for, if one may generalize, not only do women submit less readily to observation than men, but also their lives are far less tested and examined by the ordinary processes of life. Often nothing tangible remains of a woman's day. The food that has been cooked is eaten, the children that have been nursed have gone out into the world. Where does the accent fall? What is the salient point for the novelist to seize upon? For the first time, this dark country is beginning to be explored in fiction; and at the same moment, a woman has also to record the changes in women's minds and habits that the opening of the professions has introduced. She has to observe how their lives are ceasing to run underground; she has to discover what new colors and shadows are showing in them now that they are exposed to the outer world.

If, then, one should try to sum up the character of women's fiction at the present moment, one would say that it is courageous; it is sincere; it keeps closely to what women feel. It is not bitter. It does not insist upon its femininity. But at the same time, a woman's book is not written as a man would write it. These qualities are much commoner than they were, and they give even to second-and third-rate work the value of truth and the interest of sincerity.

We may expect that the office of gadfly to the state, which has been so far a male prerogative, will now be discharged by women also. Their novels will deal with social evils and remedies. Their men and women will not be observed wholly in relation to each other emotionally, but as they cohere and clash in groups and classes and races. That is one change of some importance. But there is another more interesting to those who prefer the butterfly to the gadfly—that is to say, the artist to the reformer. The greater impersonality of women's lives will encourage the poetic spirit, and it is in poetry that women's fiction is still weakest.

It will lead them to be less absorbed in facts and no longer content to record with astonishing acuteness the minute details that fall under their own observation. They will look beyond the personal and political relationships to the wider questions that the poet tries to solve—of our destiny and the meaning of life.

The basis of the poetic attitude is of course largely founded upon material things. It depends upon leisure and a little money, and the chance that money and leisure give to observe impersonally and dispassionately. With money and leisure at their service, women will naturally occupy themselves more than has hitherto been possible with the craft of letters. They will make a fuller and more subtle use of the instrument of writing. Their technique will become bolder and richer. In the future, granted time and books and a little space in the house for themselves, literature will become for women, as for men, an art to be studied.

So, if we may prophesize, women in times to come will write fewer novels but better novels; and not novels only, but poetry and criticism and history. But in this, to be sure, one is looking ahead to that golden, that perhaps fabulous age when women will have what has so long been denied them—leisure and money, and rooms to themselves.

Discussion Evaluation Form

The items below are discussion dynamics that may or may not be present in your group. Decide to what extent you think that each dynamic was present in the discussion. Then decide whether you think the group needs to work to improve in this area.

	None Some Great deal	Need to Improve?
Dominance by some individuals	1 2 3 4 5 6 7 8 9 10	Yes ❑ No ❑
Cooperation	1 2 3 4 5 6 7 8 9 10	Yes ❑ No ❑
Silence	1 2 3 4 5 6 7 8 9 10	Yes ❑ No ❑
Interrupting	1 2 3 4 5 6 7 8 9 10	Yes ❑ No ❑
Respect	1 2 3 4 5 6 7 8 9 10	Yes ❑ No ❑
Balanced participation	1 2 3 4 5 6 7 8 9 10	Yes ❑ No ❑
Active listening	1 2 3 4 5 6 7 8 9 10	Yes ❑ No ❑
Lack of interest	1 2 3 4 5 6 7 8 9 10	Yes ❑ No ❑
Asking one other questions	1 2 3 4 5 6 7 8 9 10	Yes ❑ No ❑
Building on one other's contributions	1 2 3 4 5 6 7 8 9 10	Yes ❑ No ❑
Many people talking at once	1 2 3 4 5 6 7 8 9 10	Yes ❑ No ❑

Pick one of the dynamics that you think the group should work to improve, and explain why.

How would you rate this discussion on a scale of 1–10? _____

15

Motives and Rationalizations

In previous sessions, we have looked at different ways to make the effort to explore what we don't understand. This effort has been directed toward understanding a foreign culture and toward understanding your fellow participants who might be making the difficult effort to articulate new and unfamiliar thoughts. There is a third effort that we need to make to enlarge what we understand. This concerns areas of thought that many in our society are convinced they are not able to comprehend—mathematics and science. Many of us, although eager to understand another person or culture, are convinced that in the realm of mathematics and science, it is not worthwhile even to make an effort. This perception creates a great divide in our society between those who believe that they can understand these subjects and those who believe they do not have the talent or natural gifts to grasp them. This difference has vast consequences because of the importance of these subjects in a world that is based on technology. However, this difference among us is not the inevitable fact that it seems to be. It is a difference that was likely created in grades six through eight in middle school, when, because of the way these subjects were taught, many of us became convinced that some of us had a natural talent that others lacked. The result of this perception is to make many of us strangers in our own world. Recognizing this fact is already a first step to correcting it.

"That's right." "That's wrong." How many times have we heard or used those expressions in mathematics or science classes? Most frequently in our everyday lives, answers are better or worse rather than right or wrong. Mathematics and science, however, appear to constitute a separate realm. In that realm, everything looks certain, there is rarely room for discussion, and asking a question more often signals confusion than curiosity. In these subjects, human motives, decisions, and choices can often appear absent.

Mathematicians and scientists realize that this picture misrepresents their subject matter. Although an important goal of mathematicians and scientists is to discover and create a field of study in which every question has an answer and every statement is supported by reasons, this finished product belies the struggles and decisions out of which these subjects take shape. The actual work of mathematicians and scientists is filled with uncertainty and with explorations that are sometimes fruitful, sometimes fruitless. Discussions among mathematicians and scientists, trying to articulate approaches and strategies that are better or worse, play an essential role in their efforts. Analogies from experience, our very human desires for beauty and simplicity, and decisions about what is more or less important pervade such discussions.

The isolation of these underlying questions and decisions from the theorems, formulas, and technical manipulations presented in textbooks makes the content of parts of algebra, number theory, logic, and calculus appear unnecessarily alien and arbitrary. This isolation is what is crucial in creating the opinion that some people can and some people cannot grasp these topics. The isolation is what conceals the fact that these subjects are deeply human activities. Mathematical activities—such as dealing with imaginary numbers like the square root of negative 3 or comparing differing infinites—either take on the merely game-like character of following seemingly arbitrary rules or take on an alien and mystical dimension that eludes our understanding. When we try to grasp an imaginary number, we find ourselves frustrated because we know no more about it than that certain rules apply. When we ask ourselves what the square root of negative 3 is, we feel unsatisfied and confused when all we can say is something like, "two of them multiplied together result in negative 3." If, however, we both broaden and deepen our investigation, we begin to demystify mathematics and humanize it. If we ask why a mathematician or scientist would take such a step, if we ask what the benefits and the costs of using imaginary numbers might be, then we enter the more recognizable realm of human goals and decisions.

Symbolic mathematics has not always been held in such high regard. If you think back on your own school experience, you might remember that at one time, almost everyone felt at ease with mathematics. Often when people are asked about this topic, they will state that they felt comfortable with geometry but got lost—or lost interest—once the study of algebra was introduced. Interestingly, this divide between geometry and algebra in many of our school experiences reflects a similar division in the evolution of the subject of mathematics itself. In ancient Greece, geometry was thought to be the model of mathematics and a fundamental step in everyone's education. Having an intelligence that equipped one to understand mathematics was a part of what it meant to be human. The symbolic and nonintuitive subject that we know as algebra only gained ascendancy over geometry starting in the seventeenth century. Prior to this time, the rudimentary algebraic techniques that had been developed were viewed as a dark art—a magical kind of tool used by conjurers to do tricks with numbers. It was René Descartes, whom we have seen in a number of influential roles in the development of our world, who led the change. By creating and showing the power of analytical geometry—a method that translates geometry into algebra, shapes into formulas—he transformed this dark art into the core of mathematics. Symbolic mathematics with its equations and variables then became the core of science—primarily physics—and the alienation that this highly symbolic form of activity imposed spread to our relationship with science.

It is interesting to consider why this move from geometry to algebra seems to make mathematics feel alien to many people. Algebra involves the manipulation of equations according to a strategy. There is little intuitive about the formulas that one encounters (in what way is $y = mx + b$ like a straight line?) or the steps that one takes. When we ask questions from within the subject matter itself about the rules we are using, the only answers seem to be more rules or strategies. It is only by looking behind or beneath the rules that we can begin to see the context in which such a method both makes sense at the broadest level and demonstrates its power. Until we begin to see these things, the whole enterprise has a game-like quality. But whereas we don't think that being good at games of a certain type bestows a rare and wonderful talent on people, we do feel that being good at mathematics and science does. This is the result of the centrality of science and mathematics in a world that is focused so heavily on technology. Exploring the central role in our society of mathematics and the science that is founded on it is especially useful for examining our presuppositions in this technological world. We need to locate the motives and rationalizations in these subjects that are concealed in textbooks and in the seemingly neutral way these subjects are often presented to us.

One way to go about accessing the thought processes underlying mathematics and science is by considering texts that open new fields in these areas. These texts expose the purposes, choices, gains, costs, and strategies that go into defining the subject matter. Here we see mathematicians and scientists carving out new regions of exploration; they enter an uncharted land where they themselves, as the first explorers, must place landmarks for others to follow. These landmarks are fashioned from their own previous experiences. Although some of this experience is with mathematics, most of it comes from experiences that are not strictly mathematical—from experiences that they share with the rest of us. By meeting them on this ground, we approach both a deeper understanding of, and a greater appreciation for, mathematics and science. We come to see these disciplines as deeply human activities.

We will start this task with the texts by Pascal and Heisenberg. Pascal gives one of the first and most influential accounts of the supposed contrast between the mathematical and the intuitive minds, a contrast that has since been built into our society and our educational system. In his piece, Heisenberg recounts a conversation with Albert Einstein about his own views on quantum mechanics. He struggles to connect what he is able to express mathematically with what he is able to express in the language of everyday experience, and he wonders what it means to "know" something that he cannot relate to his experience in any way. Yet he feels sure that what he knows only through mathematical models is somehow true. The question with which Heisenberg and Einstein are grappling is one of the great questions we must all face if we hope to understand the forces that shape our world.

Worksheet 15

In the unit's introduction, we explore the common perception that mathematics and science are realms, apart from everyday human experience, in which only certain people can excel. We also explore the perception that these subjects are areas in which judgment and decision-making have no part. The selections from Pascal suggests what some of the characteristics of a more mathematical, as opposed to a more intuitive, approach to the world might be. In the Heisenberg text, we listen in as two of the greatest scientists of our time grapple with ways to comprehend and express scientific truth. The worksheet asks us to consider whether various professions draw more on the "mathematical" or the "intuitive" characteristics of mind.

1. People often state that mathematicians and scientists think differently from poets and artists. Let us assume this distinction for the moment. Arrange the professionals listed below along this spectrum, placing those who think more like mathematicians on the math/science end of the spectrum, and those who think more like artists or poets on the other end.

   math/science_____ art/poetry

   a) Architect
   b) Baseball manager
   c) Doctor
   d) Journalist
   e) Lawyer
   f) Discussion leader
   g) Musician

2. Explain why you placed "doctor" where you did.

3. Explain why you placed "discussion leader" where you did.

4. Do you believe that there is a fundamental difference between people who are good at mathematics and people who are not? Why or why not?

5. After reading the texts, write an opening question for the discussion.

How Mathematical and Intuitive Minds Differ
by Blaise Pascal

The principles the mathematical mind grasps are obvious. However, they are not the ones we daily and ordinarily use. So, because of our longstanding habits, it is very hard to turn our minds in that direction. However, once we do direct our attention to them, ever so little, we understand the principles fully. And then one's mind must be very careless to reason incorrectly from principles so plain that it is almost impossible not to grasp them.

The intuitive mind finds its principles in common daily experience. They are, in fact, in front of everyone. One has only to look, and no effort is required. One only needs good eyesight, but it must be very sharp. For the principles are so subtle and numerous that it is almost impossible that we see all of them. And if we miss one principle, we will make mistakes. So one must have exceptional sight to see all the principles and then an accurate mind not to reach false conclusions from them.

All mathematicians would be intuitive if they had sharp vision. For they reason accurately from principles they know. On the other hand, intuitive minds would be mathematical if they turned their eyes toward the very general mathematical principles they don't confront in their daily activities. The reason that some intuitive minds are not mathematical is that they can't turn their attention to the principles of mathematics. But the reason mathematicians are not intuitive is that they don't see what's in front of them.

Mathematicians are accustomed to very exact and simple principles. They don't reason well until they have carefully inspected and arranged them. They are therefore lost in matters of intuition, where the principles cannot be ordered. In fact, these principles are scarcely seen. It is more accurate to say we feel them rather than see them. And it's almost impossible to get those who don't feel the principles themselves to notice them. These principles are so fine and so numerous that your senses must be very delicate and clear to grasp them. And then drawing a conclusion from them is even harder because these conclusions can't be exactly demonstrated or proven as in mathematics. This is because these principles aren't known to us in the same way and because the proofs would be infinite. We must seize the conclusions at once, in one glance, and not primarily by a process of reasoning.

So it's very rare to find a mathematician who is intuitive, or an intuitive mind that is mathematical. Mathematicians make themselves ridiculous because they want to treat matters of intuition mathematically. They want to begin with definitions and axioms, but such a procedure is completely inappropriate when applied to our daily experiences and activities. It isn't that the mind doesn't do this, but it does it naturally and immediately, and without any technical rules of reasoning. The description of this sort of reasoning is beyond all of us, and only a few can feel it.

Intuitive minds, on the other hand, judge at a single glance. They are therefore astonished when they are presented with mathematical propositions and theorems that they don't understand. In addition, when they are told that these theorems can only be approached through definitions and axioms that seem to them sterile and unnecessarily detailed, they are repelled and disheartened.

But dull minds are neither intuitive nor mathematical. Mathematicians who are only mathematical have exact minds as long as everything is explained to them by means of definitions and axioms. Otherwise they are inaccurate and insufferable. They are only right when the principles are entirely clear. And intuitive minds that are only intuitive don't have the patience to reach the very first principles of things. They therefore can't grasp the foundations of purely speculative and conceptual matters, which they have never seen in the world and which are beyond their daily experience.

On What People Are
by Blaise Pascal

No one is recognized in the world as skilled at poetry unless he or she has put up a sign announcing himself or herself as a poet. No one is recognized as good at mathematics unless they declare themselves to be mathematicians. But people who have really been educated don't want signs and labels. Educated people are not poets or mathematicians. They are all these, and judges of all these. No one guesses what they are. When they come into a group, they participate in whatever is being discussed. You don't notice one ability or skill in them rather than another, except when they have to use it. But then we notice it. It is typical of such people that we don't call them fine speakers, when giving a speech is not at issue. But when it is, we say they are fine speakers. It is a very false kind of praise to describe someone as a clever poet when they enter a room. But it is a very bad sign when someone is not called upon to give an opinion and judge a poem.

A Talk with Einstein about Atomic Physics
by Werner Heisenberg

In the spring of 1926, I was invited to talk to the physics department at the University of Berlin about new theories in atomic physics. Since this was my first chance to meet some of the most famous physicists of the time, I was careful to speak very clearly about my ideas on atomic physics, which were then considered very unusual. I apparently managed to interest Einstein, for he invited me to walk home with him so we might discuss these ideas more fully.

On the way, he asked me about my research. As soon as we were indoors, he turned the conversation to a question that focused on the philosophical background of my work. "What you have told us sounds very strange. You assume, quite rightly, that electrons exist inside the atom. But you refuse to admit that they move in orbits around the nucleus of the atom, like the planets around the sun. You do this even though we can observe the tracks electrons leave as they pass through cloud chambers—an observation that is usually accepted as evidence that electrons move in orbits."

"I have a strong suspicion that, on account of the problems we have been discussing, your theory will one day get you into hot water. I will explain this further," said Einstein. "When it comes to observation and reporting the results of experiments, you act as if you can use ordinary language in the ordinary way. You do this when you say that you can observe the path of an electron in a cloud chamber, even though, as you know, the electrons in a cloud chamber are not contained inside an atom. But at the same time, you claim that there are no orbits. You can't get rid of the electron paths that easily."

I tried to come to the defense of the new atomic physics. "For the time being," I said, "we don't know what language to use to talk about what happens inside the atom. We have a mathematical language in which we can express, for example, the amount of energy an atom contains at a certain time, and also the probability that the atoms will lose this energy. But we don't know how this mathematical language relates to the ordinary language we all speak. And we need to know this if we are to apply our theory to our experience. This is because we can only describe our experiments in ordinary language, not in mathematical language. Therefore, I know that I don't really understand modern atomic physics. But what I do know is that the mathematical part of the theory works, and I know how to describe the experiments in ordinary language. What I don't know is how to put the two together." "Very well, I will accept that," Einstein said. "But perhaps I may put another question to you. How can you really have so much faith in your theory when, as you admit, so many crucial problems remain completely unsolved?"

I must have thought for a very long time before I produced my answer. "I believe, just like you, that the simplicity of natural laws is a sign of their truth. If nature leads us to mathematical theories of great simplicity and beauty, we cannot help thinking that they are true, that they reveal a real part of nature. I admit that these mathematical theories may also reflect elements of our own thinking. But the mere fact that we could never have thought them up by ourselves means that they were revealed to us by nature. This suggests strongly that they must be part of reality itself, not just of our thoughts about reality. Therefore, though the objections you raise have merit, and though I realize that at the moment I must contradict myself in expressing my theory, I have no doubt that I am correct."

Discussion Evaluation Form

The items below are discussion dynamics that may or may not be present in your group. Decide to what extent you think that each dynamic was present in the discussion. Then decide whether you think the group needs to work to improve in this area.

	None Some Great deal	Need to Improve?
Dominance by some individuals	1 2 3 4 5 6 7 8 9 10	Yes ❑ No ❑
Cooperation	1 2 3 4 5 6 7 8 9 10	Yes ❑ No ❑
Silence	1 2 3 4 5 6 7 8 9 10	Yes ❑ No ❑
Interrupting	1 2 3 4 5 6 7 8 9 10	Yes ❑ No ❑
Respect	1 2 3 4 5 6 7 8 9 10	Yes ❑ No ❑
Balanced participation	1 2 3 4 5 6 7 8 9 10	Yes ❑ No ❑
Active listening	1 2 3 4 5 6 7 8 9 10	Yes ❑ No ❑
Lack of interest	1 2 3 4 5 6 7 8 9 10	Yes ❑ No ❑
Asking one other questions	1 2 3 4 5 6 7 8 9 10	Yes ❑ No ❑
Building on one other's contributions	1 2 3 4 5 6 7 8 9 10	Yes ❑ No ❑
Many people talking at once	1 2 3 4 5 6 7 8 9 10	Yes ❑ No ❑

Pick one of the dynamics that you think the group should work to improve, and explain why.

How would you rate this discussion on a scale of 1–10? _____

Participant Questionnaire

In the best discussions, each person acts simultaneously as a participant and a leader. Furthermore, each group member acts with the interests of the group in mind and governs his or her participation accordingly. This self-evaluation form helps you reflect on your participation and recognize areas in which you would like to improve.

How much would you say that you participate?

❑ Less than most   ❑ About average   ❑ More than most

How often do you interrupt others?

❑ Very Little   ❑ Sometimes   ❑ Often   ❑ All the time

How often do you listen to all the participants?

❑ Very Little   ❑ Sometimes   ❑ Often   ❑ All the time

How often do you solicit other opinions?

❑ Very Little   ❑ Sometimes   ❑ Often   ❑ All the time

How often do you build on what others say?

❑ Very Little   ❑ Sometimes   ❑ Often   ❑ All the time

How often do you keep focused and on task?

❑ Very Little   ❑ Sometimes   ❑ Often   ❑ All the time

How often do you encourage quieter participants to speak?

❑ Very Little   ❑ Sometimes   ❑ Often   ❑ All the time

How often do you prepare well for the sessions?

❑ Very Little   ❑ Sometimes   ❑ Often   ❑ All the time

What is one way in which you have improved as a participant?

Name one way that you would like to improve as a participant.

Stage 4

Leadership, Participation, and Commitment

16

Becoming Ourselves

Most of us have in mind a goal or direction for ourselves. We seek to develop ourselves or, paradoxically, to become ourselves. We hope to attain some vision that we may feel is implicit in us, or completes us, or gives meaning to the various aspects of our lives. Some people do this through study or work. Others seek to fulfill themselves through a pilgrimage to a special place or by finding a partner or mentor. Still others seek themselves through meditation or artistic creativity. In the three previous stages of *Mapping the Future*, we also have been changing and becoming ourselves, but in two ways—as individuals and as a group. As individuals, we had to learn to discern our individual strengths and weaknesses and to discover who could help us and whom we could assist; as a group, we have had to overcome the cultural presuppositions we have inherited that have kept us from being genuinely open with one another. As we move through this final stage of *Mapping the Future*, the changes that we have undergone as individuals and as a group will move closer together and become interdependent.

One of the ways in which we can experience the growing interdependence of the changes we have undergone is through the evolving nature of our experience of leadership. In the first stage, we explored and modified the role of the traditional expert and teacher. We began to speak with one another without the mediation of someone who determined whether what we said was correct or interesting. This was a significant change in our habits and expectations. It began to seem feasible that a group of people, none of whom were experts on a specific topic, could have interesting and important things to say to one another. The second stage took this new attitude a step further. We went beyond the belief that some people could offer important insights and opinions to the realization that all people could. We began to view people as possessing a variety of skills—or what is sometimes called forms of intelligence—that require the help of others to truly come to fruition. We realized that the contributions of each of us were needed to reach a deeper level of complexity and texture in our consideration of all the important issues we face. In the third stage, we began to focus on ourselves. We had to examine and evaluate our presuppositions, and struggle to overcome the ways in which these become impediments to our attempts to understand others. Although we will continue to work on these skills, attitudes, and expectations, we are now moving on to the next stage. In this stage, as we reflect more deliberately on the perspective and practice of leadership, all our previous accomplishments will be brought into play and refined.

Leadership is often seen as the defining trait of a particular sort of person. Alexander the Great, Napoleon, Abraham Lincoln, Martin Luther King Jr., Joan of Arc, and Gandhi, among many others, are often considered historical models of leadership. In our society, chief executives of corporations are often pointed to as leaders. An increasing number of books and courses of study help rising managers and prospective company presidents investigate what it means to be a leader. A leader, we are told, is a commander, a visionary, a motivator, a source of inspiration, a model, an explorer, a teacher, a charismatic person, a hero, and the list goes on. No matter how we define leaders and leadership, we at least tend to agree that there are leaders. Our organizations and social structures are built around leaders. Leaders, we tend to believe, cause things to happen.

However, during the course of *Mapping the Future*, we have been examining and modifying our traditional concepts of leadership and the power that accompanies it. A Touchstones Discussion leader is not someone who shows others the way through a terrain that the leader has already traversed. Rather, the leader is someone who must conduct a discussion on a subject and texts on which he or she has no particular claim to expertise. The leader therefore must practice speaking responsibly in a situation of high uncertainty and also make it possible for others to do the same. In addition, a leader must practice listening. Nothing is more destructive to a leader's credibility than to misstate another person's comment or impose a personal agenda on another person's words. And lastly, a leader must always be ready to surrender the position of leadership to other individuals in the group or to the group as a whole. In fact, the leader's ultimate goal should be to come to a situation in which all members of the group are acting simultaneously as leaders and participants and sharing responsibility for the shape of the discussion. From the start of this discussion program, we have been experimenting with different forms of leadership that required each of us to be alternately a leader and a follower. At first, this alternating approach may have been confusing and perhaps even frustrating. The *Leader's Supplement* itself may have served as a de facto leader, an authority to which all the participants deferred. But gradually the group should have been able to use it simply as a guide on a journey, the success for which all the participants had to take some responsibility. As each participant took ownership in the group, the group members began to move from being alternately leaders and participants to being simultaneously leaders and participants. And as the role of leader has become more essentially a part of each participant's role, we have become able to compose our own guide for the discussion.

In this unit, as we think about the changes we have been through together and separately, we will consider a pair of texts that present two different approaches to fundamental personal change. One author, Saint Theresa Ávila, deals with the difficulties one faces as one tries to move closer to God through prayer. She describes how one starts to pray and how one overcomes and deals with the feelings of emptiness and barrenness in the early stages of praying. She then describes how one moves through the next three stages as prayer becomes more natural. Shunryu Suzuki describes a very different approach. Rather than attempt to move closer to God, the practitioner of Zen attempts to achieve enlightenment by being entirely in the present. For Suzuki, any external purpose or goal-directedness defeats the attempt to meditate and inhabit the present. Suzuki describes four stages of meditation—not as developmental steps but rather as different levels of good practice. The two approaches are different with respect to the process we move through in creating a discussion group, yet might supply interesting analogies for what we are attempting.

Session Strategy Worksheet

1. **Goals.** Consider the strengths and weaknesses of previous discussions and the progress of your group as a whole. What would you like for the group to accomplish in your session? Are there specific problems that need to be addressed, or perhaps a new skill that needs to be developed, or an issue that should be examined? Taking into account the texts as well as the history and needs of your group, what do you think would be important for the group to consider about these texts? Why?

2. **Handouts.** Will you have everyone complete a handout? If so, on a separate sheet, compose the handout that you will present. Will the participants complete the handout during the session, or do you need to distribute it before the session so that the participants can complete it in advance? Will you reserve any time in the session for a discussion of the handout? Will that time come before or after the general discussion?

3. **Small Group Work.** Will you have any small group work? If so, what will you have the groups do? Should the small group work come before or after the general discussion? Will you have the small groups report results to the larger group?

4. **Large Group Discussion.** How will you start the general discussion? Will you ask an opening question? Will you ask everyone to prepare and present an opening question? Or will you plan to move naturally from the reports of the small groups or consideration of the handout into the discussion? If you plan to ask an opening question, what will it be?

5. **Troubleshooting.** What problems do you anticipate may arise in the discussion of these texts? How might you plan to address such problems?

6. **Evaluations.** Will you have the participants fill out an evaluation sheet as part of the session? Will you reserve any part of the session for the group members to talk about the strengths and weaknesses of the session and discussion?

On Learning How to Pray

by Saint Theresa Ávila

The beginner in prayer must think of himself as setting out to make a garden in poor soil filled with weeds. In this garden, the Lord is to take His delight. God weeds the garden and puts good plants in their place. Suppose this has already happened. In other words, we have determined to practice prayer and have already started. With God's help, we must now become good gardeners and make our plants grow. We must water them carefully so that they will not die but produce flowers. The plants will smell sweetly and refresh our Lord. He will often come into our garden to take his pleasure and delight among these flowers that are our virtues.

Let us now consider how this garden can be watered. That way we will know what we must do, how much work it will take, and for how long we must work if the gain will be greater than the effort. It seems to me that the garden can be watered in four ways. We can take water from a well by hand, though that is hard work for us. We can get water by a waterwheel and bucket that is powered by a pump. I have sometimes gotten water this second way. It is easier than getting it by hand and also delivers more water. Third, we can get it from a stream or brook that runs through the garden. This waters the ground much better. There is no need to water it as often, and the gardener's work is much less. The last way to water a garden is by a heavy rain. Then the Lord waters it. This way costs us no work at all and is by far the best way. These four ways of watering a garden stand for the four degrees of prayer that the Lord, in His goodness, has occasionally brought to my soul. Now I will talk about the first way of getting water, drawing it out by hand, which corresponds to beginning to learn to pray. Beginners in prayer, we may say, are those who draw the water from the well by hand. It exhausts us because we are used to a life of pleasure. In starting to pray, we are similarly exhausted by trying to keep our senses under control. This is very difficult, since we are used to spending all our time distracting ourselves by means of our senses. Beginners in prayer must pay no attention to what they see or hear. We must practice this during our hours of prayer. We must go away by ourselves and, while alone, think over our past life. In fact, we must all do this whether we are at the beginning of the road or near its end. However, there are differences about how much it must be done.

At first, thinking about our past life causes distress. For beginners are not always sure that they have repented for their sins. This uncertainty is present even though they have repented as we can see because they have, at least, determined to serve God so faithfully. Then also they have to try to think about the life of Christ, and this effort tires their minds. We can make this much progress by ourselves—though, even then, this progress needs God's help, since without God's help, we can't think a single good thought.

Mistakes in Practice
by Shunryu Suzuki

There are several ways of poor practice that you should understand. Usually when you practice sitting in meditation, you become very goal-oriented. You set up an ideal or goal that you strive to attain and fulfill. But as I have often said, this is absurd. When you are driven by a goal, you have some driving idea within yourself. But by the time you attain your goal, you will immediately create another one. So as long as your practice is based on a driving idea, and you practice sitting in a goal-directed way, you will have no time to actually attain your goal. Moreover, you will be sacrificing the meat of your practice. Because your attainment is always ahead, you will always be sacrificing yourself now for some ideal in the future. You end up with nothing. This is absurd; it is not adequate practice at all. But even worse than this goal-driven attitude is to practice sitting and meditating in competition with someone else. This is a poor, shabby kind of practice.

Even when you practice sitting alone, without a teacher, I think you will find some way to tell whether your practice is adequate or not. When you are tired of sitting, or when you are disgusted with your practice, you should recognize this as a warning signal. You become discouraged with your practice when your practice has become set toward a goal. You have some ruling idea driving practice, and it is not pure enough. It is when your practice is rather greedy that you become discouraged with it. So you should be grateful that you have a sign or warning signal to show you the weak point in your practice. At that time, forgetting all about your mistake and renewing your way, you can resume your original practice. This is a very important point.

So as long as you continue your practice, you are quite safe. But as it is very difficult to continue, you must find some way to encourage yourself. As it is hard to encourage yourself without becoming involved in some poor kind of practice, to continue our pure practice by yourself may be rather difficult. This is why we have a teacher. With your teacher, you will correct your practice. Of course you will have a very hard time with him, but even so, you will always be safe from wrong practice.

Most Zen Buddhist priests have had a difficult time with their masters. When they talk about the difficulties, you may think that without this kind of hardship you cannot practice meditating. But this is not true. Whether you have difficulties in your practice or not, as long as you continue it, you have pure practice in its true sense. Even when you are not aware of it, you have it. So Dogen-zenji said, "Do not think you will necessarily be aware of your own enlightenment." Whether or not you are aware of it, you have your own true enlightenment within your practice.

Another mistake will be to practice for the sake of the joy you find in it. Actually, when your practice is involved in a feeling of joy, it is not in very good shape either. Of course this is not poor practice, but compared to the true practice it is not so good. In Hinayana Buddhism, practice is classified in four ways. The best way is just to do it without having any joy in it, not even spiritual joy. This way is just to do it, forgetting your physical and mental feeling, forgetting all about yourself in your practice. This is the fourth stage, or the highest stage. The next highest stage is to have just physical joy in your practice. At this stage, you find some pleasure in practice, and you will practice because of the pleasure you find in it. In the second stage, you have both mental and physical joy, or good feeling. These two middle stages are stages in which you practice meditating because you feel good in your practice. The first stage is all the stages we mentioned earlier, to practice for a goal, or to compete. These four stages also apply to our Mahayana practice, and the highest is just to practice it.

And if you want to find some encouragement in your discouragement, getting tired of practice is itself the encouragement. You encourage yourself when you get tired of it. When you do not want to do it, that is the warning signal. It is like having a toothache when your teeth are not so good. When you feel some pain in your teeth, you go to the dentist. That is our way.

The cause of conflict is some fixed idea or one-sided idea. If you understand the cause of conflict as some fixed or one-sided idea, you can find meaning in various practices without being caught by any of them. If you do not realize this point, you will be easily caught by some particular way, and you will say, "This is enlightenment! This is perfect practice. This is our way. The rest of the ways are not perfect. This is the best way." This is a big mistake. There is no particular way in true practice. You should find your own way, and you should know what kind of practice you have right now. Knowing both the advantages and disadvantages of some special practice, you can practice that special way without danger. But if you have a one-sided attitude, you will ignore the disadvantage of the practice, emphasizing only its good part. Eventually you will discover the worst side of the practice and become discouraged when it is too late. This is silly. We should be grateful that the ancient teachers point out this mistake.

Discussion Evaluation Form

The items below are discussion dynamics that may or may not be present in your group. Decide to what extent you think that each dynamic was present in the discussion. Then decide whether you think the group needs to work to improve in this area.

	None Some Great deal	Need to Improve?
Dominance by some individuals	1 2 3 4 5 6 7 8 9 10	Yes ❑ No ❑
Cooperation	1 2 3 4 5 6 7 8 9 10	Yes ❑ No ❑
Silence	1 2 3 4 5 6 7 8 9 10	Yes ❑ No ❑
Interrupting	1 2 3 4 5 6 7 8 9 10	Yes ❑ No ❑
Respect	1 2 3 4 5 6 7 8 9 10	Yes ❑ No ❑
Balanced participation	1 2 3 4 5 6 7 8 9 10	Yes ❑ No ❑
Active listening	1 2 3 4 5 6 7 8 9 10	Yes ❑ No ❑
Lack of interest	1 2 3 4 5 6 7 8 9 10	Yes ❑ No ❑
Asking one other questions	1 2 3 4 5 6 7 8 9 10	Yes ❑ No ❑
Building on one other's contributions	1 2 3 4 5 6 7 8 9 10	Yes ❑ No ❑
Many people talking at once	1 2 3 4 5 6 7 8 9 10	Yes ❑ No ❑

Pick one of the dynamics that you think the group should work to improve, and explain why.

How would you rate this discussion on a scale of 1–10? _____

Strategy Evaluation Worksheet

1. How would you rate the discussion on a scale of 1 to 10, with 1 being least successful and 10 being most successful? Why?

2. What did the leaders do that differed from your strategy for this session?

3. What was the opening question? Do you think it was a good question? Why or why not?

4. What topics were not raised that you thought should have been?

5. Are there things the leaders did not do that you think they should have?

6. Are there things the leaders did do that you think they should not have?

17

The Individual and Community

Throughout *Mapping the Future*, we have been exploring what it means to be both an individual and a member of a group or community. Each of us runs the risk of either asserting our individuality excessively and dominating others or minimizing our individuality so much that we are entirely absorbed as a member of a group. Striking the appropriate balance—between respect for our own and others' individuality and sensitivity to the needs and dynamics of the whole group—has been of the essence in our task of forming a group capable of genuine discussion.

We can find accounts of the tension between individuality and the needs of the group in some of the earliest documents of Western culture. Homer's *Iliad* revolves around the wrath Achilles feels when he must subordinate his own status to the structure of the group—when he must surrender his prize for valor, a woman, to his king, Agamemnon, so that Agamemnon may retain his stature as the ruler of the Greek warriors before Troy. We see a similar tension in the passages in the Bible in which Joseph and his brothers struggle to find some balance between his greatness as the vice-ruler of Egypt and his position in the family. In more recent times, the U.S. Bill of Rights testifies to the ongoing tension between the rights of the individual and the demands of the community.

Although the tension between self and society is a perennial issue within the culture of the West, our sense of self has evolved considerably over time. The extension of the voting franchise in the United States to people other than white male landowners reflected the emerging recognition of all people as full and individual selves. Our sense of individuality can vary with not only time but also social location. There are certain people within most communities who, because of their position, surrender much of their individuality in the sense that for them, there can be no purely personal action—every action and moment has significance within the structure of the society. This idea was famously and succinctly articulated by King Louis the XIV of France in the phrase, "L'Etat, c'est moi," which translates as "I am the state."

Another example of the variability of our sense of individuality can be seen in the ways in which marks of our uniqueness have been interpreted socially. In contemporary Western society, for example, each of us has a characteristic handwritten signature. It is a distinguishing mark that separates us from every other person. We attach both legal and moral significance to the idea of "signing on" to something; when we sign our names, we are in some way investing our selves. However, in mid-sixteenth-century England, only one person's signature was assumed to be the same each time it appeared. That person was Queen Elizabeth I. Her unique signature was something that appertained to her as queen, not simply as a person. The name of her famous contemporary Shakespeare, conversely, appears with a wide variety of configurations and spellings. Later editors, responding to a custom that had developed in their own time to attach a particular signature to a single individual, regularized the spelling of Shakespeare's name that we use today.

In thinking about this session as a leader, you will be dealing with these same issues of tension between the individual and the community, between the person and the social role he or she inhabits. You will not be able to view your group either as a mere collection of individuals or as an organic whole made up of inseparable parts. Rather, you must view the group as composed of specific people, each with specific strengths and weaknesses and interests and aversions. The individuality of a participant can be lost or overlooked in a discussion group in all sorts of ways—for example, when we interrupt another person, refuse to respond to her ideas, or refuse to allow him the validity of his perspective. Conversely, the good of the group can be sacrificed to the excesses of one or two individuals who, knowingly or not, use the discussion to further a particular agenda or express their ideas to a captive audience. It is a leader's task to always be attuned to such possibilities and to help each member of the group both engage with the discussion on an individual level and contribute from his or her unique perspective something valuable for the whole group. As you concentrate on achieving this goal, you might find it helpful to discuss the topic of individuality explicitly through this unit's texts. One text is abstract and philosophical; the other is very specific and recounts a decisive moment in a young person's life.

In the selection from *Leviathan*, Thomas Hobbes explores the question of what we are like in our essence as individuals—that is, what we would be like completely alone, apart from any society. He does not imagine that we would ever exist in such a situation, but he does believe that one cannot fully understand the nature of society itself or the ongoing tension between society and the individual without understanding what our nature as individuals consists of. Hobbes holds that outside society, in the "state of nature," we are essentially competitive creatures, giving heed only to our own desires. We move into society simply to ensure our security. Without the safety that society brings, our lives are, in his famous phrase, "solitary, nasty, brutish, and short." We give up some freedom as individuals in order to be able to sleep peacefully. The group members should consider whether they agree with Hobbes's estimation of our essential natures as solitary and competitive. What sort of evidence would you bring either to support or dispute such a claim? How does one's feeling about such an issue color the ways in which one views society and our interactions with one another? The text by Malcolm X deals with another aspect of the issue, told from the concrete perspective of his autobiography. He tells a story about a moment as an eighth-grade student when he was viewed not as an individual but as a part of a group. He claims this event marked a decisive point in his life because his possibilities were viewed as entirely circumscribed by history and race and he was invited to see himself as this person saw him. Such moments, when we suddenly realize that another person is unable to see us as the person whom we feel we are, can be very painful for all of us. It will be important for the members of the group to reflect on what sort of loss they feel when suddenly their individuality and uniqueness is stripped away from them by other people, by society, or by indifference to their specific perspective or contribution—in other words, how they feel when they are seen merely as one among many.

Session Strategy Worksheet

1. **Goals.** Consider the strengths and weaknesses of previous discussions and the progress of your group as a whole. What would you like for the group to accomplish in your session? Are there specific problems that need to be addressed, or perhaps a new skill that needs to be developed, or an issue that should be examined? Taking into account the texts as well as the history and needs of your group, what do you think would be important for the group to consider about these texts? Why?

2. **Handouts.** Will you have everyone complete a handout? If so, on a separate sheet, compose the handout that you will present. Will the participants complete the handout during the session, or do you need to distribute it before the session so that the participants can complete it in advance? Will you reserve any time in the session for a discussion of the handout? Will that time come before or after the general discussion?

3. **Small Group Work.** Will you have any small group work? If so, what will you have the groups do? Should the small group work come before or after the general discussion? Will you have the small groups report results to the larger group?

4. **Large Group Discussion.** How will you start the general discussion? Will you ask an opening question? Will you ask everyone to prepare and present an opening question? Or will you plan to move naturally from the reports of the small groups or consideration of the handout into the discussion? If you plan to ask an opening question, what will it be?

5. **Troubleshooting.** What problems do you anticipate may arise in the discussion of these texts? How might you plan to address such problems?

6. **Evaluations.** Will you have the participants fill out an evaluation sheet as part of the session? Will you reserve any part of the session for the group members to talk about the strengths and weaknesses of the session and discussion?

Leviathan

by Thomas Hobbes

Men by nature equal: Nature has made men so equal in the faculties of the body and mind that, when all is reckoned together, though there be found one man sometimes manifestly stronger in body or of quicker mind than another, yet the difference between man and man is not enough that any man can claim to himself any benefit to which another man cannot pretend as well as he. For as to the strength of body, the weakest has strength enough to kill the strongest, either by secret machination or by confederacy with others that are in the same danger with himself.

From equality proceeds fear: From this equality of ability arises equality of hope in the attaining of our ends. And therefore if any two men desire the same thing, which nevertheless they cannot both enjoy, they become enemies. In the way to their goal that is principally their own conservation or preservation, and sometimes their pleasure only, they endeavor to destroy or subdue one another. And from hence it comes to pass that whenever a potential invader has no more to fear than another man's single power, if the latter plant, sow, build, or possess a convenient residence, that invader may probably be expected to come prepared with forces united to dispossess and deprive him, not only of the fruit of his labor, but also of his life or liberty. And the invader again is in the like danger from another.

From fear war: And from this fear of one another there is no way for any man to secure himself so reasonably as by anticipation—that is, by force or wiles to master the persons of all men he can, until he sees no power left that is great enough to endanger him. This is no more than his own conservation requires, and is generally allowed.

Moreover, every man desires that others should value him at the same rate he sets upon himself; and upon all signs of contempt or undervaluing he naturally endeavors, as far as he dares, to extort a greater value from those who have contempt for him by force, and from others by that example.

So that in the nature of man we find three principal causes of quarrel: first, competition; second, fear; third, glory.

Without a state, there is always war of every one against every one: Hereby it is manifest that, during the time men live without a common power to keep them all in awe, they are in that condition that is called war, and such a war is of every man against every man. For war consists not in battle only, or the act of fighting, but in a period of time wherein the will to contend by battle is sufficiently known. Therefore the notion of *time* is to be considered in the nature of war as it is in the nature of weather. For as the nature of foul weather lies not in a shower or two of rain but in a continued threat of rain for many days together, so the nature of war consists not in actual fighting but in the known disposition to it during all the time there is no assurance to the contrary. All other time is peace.

The bad consequences of such war: Whatsoever, therefore, is a consequence of a time of war where every man is enemy to every man, the same is consequent to the time when men live without other security than what their own strength and their own invention shall furnish them. In such a condition, there is no place for industry, because the fruit thereof is uncertain—and consequently no culture of the earth; no navigation nor use of the commodities that may be imported by sea; no permanent building, no instruments of moving and removing such things as require much force; no knowledge of the face of the earth; no account of time; no arts; no letters; no society; and, which is worst of all, continual fear and danger of violent death. The life of man is solitary, poor, nasty, brutish, and short.

The Autobiography of Malcolm X
by Malcolm X

I continued to think constantly about all that I had seen in Boston and about the way I had felt there. I know now that it was the sense of being a real part of a mass of my own kind, for the first time.

The white people—my classmates, the Swerlins, the people at the restaurant where I worked—noticed the change. They said, "You're acting so strange. You don't seem like yourself, Malcolm. What's the matter?" I kept close to the top of the class, though. The topmost scholastic standing, I remember, kept shifting between me, a girl named Audrey Slaugh, and a boy named Jimmy Cotton. It went on that way, as I became increasingly restless and disturbed through the first semester. And then one day, just about when those of us who had passed were about to move up to 8-A, from which we would enter high school the next year, something happened that was to become the first major turning point of my life.

Somehow I happened to be alone in the classroom with Mr. Ostrowski, my English teacher. He was a tall, rather reddish white man, and he had a thick mustache. I had gotten some of my best marks under him, and he had always made me feel that he liked me. He was a natural-born "adviser" about what you ought to read, do, or think—about anything and everything. We used to make unkind jokes about him. Why was he teaching in Mason instead of somewhere else, getting for himself some of the "success in life" that he kept telling us how to get?

I know that he probably meant well in what he happened to advise me that day. I doubt that he meant any harm. It was just in his nature as an American white man. I was one of his top students, one the school's top students—but all he could see for me was the kind of future "in your place" that almost all white people see for black people.

He told me, "Malcolm, you ought to be thinking about a career. Have you been giving it thought?" The truth is, I hadn't. I never have figured out why I told him, "Well, yes, sir, I've been thinking I'd like to be a lawyer." In those days, Lansing certainly had no Negro lawyers—or doctors either—to hold up an image I might have aspired to. All I really knew for certain was that a lawyer didn't wash dishes, as I was doing.

Mr. Ostrowski looked surprised, I remember, and leaned back in his chair and clasped his hands behind his head. He kind of half-smiled and said, "Malcolm, one of life's first needs is for us to be realistic about being a nigger. A lawyer—that's no realistic goal for a nigger. You need to think about something you can be. You're good with your hands—making things. Everybody admires your carpentry shop work. Why don't you plan on carpentry? People like you as a person—you'd get all kinds of work."

The more I thought afterward about what he said, the more uneasy it made me. It just kept treading around in my mind. What made it really begin to disturb me was Mr. Ostrowski's advice to others in my class—all of them white. Most of them had told him they were planning to become farmers, like their parents—to one day take over their family farms. But those who wanted to strike out on their own, to try something new, he had encouraged. Some, mostly girls, wanted to be teachers. A few wanted other professions, such as one boy who wanted to become a county agent; another, a veterinarian; and one girl wanted to be a nurse. They all reported that Mr. Ostrowski had encouraged whatever they had wanted. Yet nearly none of them had earned marks equal to mine.

It was then that I began to change—inside.

I drew away from white people. I came to class, and I answered when called upon. But it became a physical strain simply to sit in Mr. Ostrowski's class.

Where "nigger" had slipped off my back before, wherever I heard it now, I stopped and looked at whoever said it. And they looked surprised that I did.

I quit hearing so much "nigger" and also "What's wrong?"—which was the way I wanted it. Nobody, including the teachers, could decide what had come over me. I knew I was being discussed. In a few more weeks, it was that way, too, at the restaurant where I worked washing dishes, and at the Swerlins'.

One day soon after, Mrs. Swerlin called me into the living room, and there was that state man, Maynard Allen. I knew from their faces that something was about to happen. She told me that none of them could understand why—after I had done so well in school, and on my job, and living with them, and after everyone in Mason had come to like me—I had lately begun to make them all feel that I wasn't happy there anymore.

She said she felt there was no need for me to stay at the detention home any longer, and that arrangements had been made for me to go and live with the Lyons family, who liked me so much. She stood up and put out her hand, "I guess I've asked you a hundred times, Malcolm—do you want to tell me what's wrong?"

I shook her hand, and said, "Nothing, Mrs. Swerlin." Then I went and got my things, and came back down. At the living room door I saw her wiping her eyes. I felt very bad. I thanked her and went out in front to Mr. Allen, who took me over to the Lyons'.

Mr. and Mrs. Lyons, and their children, during the two months I lived with them—while finishing eighth grade—also tried to get me to tell them what was wrong. But somehow I couldn't tell them either.

Discussion Evaluation Form

The items below are discussion dynamics that may or may not be present in your group. Decide to what extent you think that each dynamic was present in the discussion. Then decide whether you think the group needs to work to improve in this area.

	None Some Great deal	Need to Improve?
Dominance by some individuals	1 2 3 4 5 6 7 8 9 10	Yes ❑ No ❑
Cooperation	1 2 3 4 5 6 7 8 9 10	Yes ❑ No ❑
Silence	1 2 3 4 5 6 7 8 9 10	Yes ❑ No ❑
Interrupting	1 2 3 4 5 6 7 8 9 10	Yes ❑ No ❑
Respect	1 2 3 4 5 6 7 8 9 10	Yes ❑ No ❑
Balanced participation	1 2 3 4 5 6 7 8 9 10	Yes ❑ No ❑
Active listening	1 2 3 4 5 6 7 8 9 10	Yes ❑ No ❑
Lack of interest	1 2 3 4 5 6 7 8 9 10	Yes ❑ No ❑
Asking one other questions	1 2 3 4 5 6 7 8 9 10	Yes ❑ No ❑
Building on one other's contributions	1 2 3 4 5 6 7 8 9 10	Yes ❑ No ❑
Many people talking at once	1 2 3 4 5 6 7 8 9 10	Yes ❑ No ❑

Pick one of the dynamics that you think the group should work to improve, and explain why.

How would you rate this discussion on a scale of 1–10? _____

Strategy Evaluation Worksheet

1. How would you rate the discussion on a scale of 1 to 10, with 1 being least successful and 10 being most successful? Why?

2. What did the leaders do that differed from your strategy for this session?

3. What was the opening question? Do you think it was a good question? Why or why not?

4. What topics were not raised that you thought should have been?

5. Are there things the leaders did not do that you think they should have?

6. Are there things the leaders did do that you think they should not have?

18

Specialization and Technology

Technology and specialization, and the mass production and efficiency they make possible, have raised the standard of living enormously over the past four centuries. However, the problems caused by technology and specialization are also significant. The earth's forests and rivers have been destroyed or transformed in ways that many people find horrifying. Our human cultural environment has also been transformed in ways that are not always positive. Consider, for example, some of the less- benign effects of specialization and the division of labor. We hear of new ailments in the workplace caused by the constant repetition of the same motion either on a production line or in an office. As important, many people feel that their real lives take place when they are not at work. For most people, work is something they try to get through. Rather than enlivening them, it seems to put their abilities on hold. Such considerations make it clear that "standard of living" and "quality of life" are not necessarily equivalent terms.

One question that might be pursued as we think about the effects of technological progress in our lives is whether the more negative aspects can be mitigated. Consider again our example of the division of labor in modern societies. We know that, for many people, working life is confined to mastering a few simple operations. There is little opportunity to learn new skills or to exercise the mind. The modern worker may become woefully ignorant. This seems most likely to be true for workers who do repetitive physical work, such as assembly-line manufacturing—but might it not also be true of the intellectual specializations that have become common? Are there significant numbers of people in our society who have not been affected by the trend toward specialization that has resulted from our modern preoccupation with efficiency? Or is work that engages the whole person something that no more than a few people will ever experience? Even people on modern university faculties are required to specialize to get promoted. What effect does doing the same exercises in thought again and again have on one's ability to take a broader perspective? Futurists often claim that specialized, rote jobs will be replaced by other forms of activity and that most repetitive tasks will ultimately be handled by machines. But although we may want to be optimistic about the future, our experience suggests that, at least from within its own frame of reference, the drive toward increased specialization imposed by a technological society is difficult to counteract.

In this unit's texts, we consider the effects of technology on people and on the environment. In "Four Who Mastered Science," a tale from India, we see a portrait of the temptation to build and try out whatever is technically possible—whether this is a new weapon or a type of genetic engineering or an artificial food or a medical procedure. Since the creation of atomic weapons, people have wondered whether technology can, and should, be controlled. The selection by Heidegger claims that technology not only leads to specialization and tempts us to play God, it also entirely transforms our relationship with the world. Things are viewed entirely as at our disposal and for our use. We look around us and see not a world so much as raw materials that we can store up and stockpile until we are ready to use them. Even the objects that technology produces from these materials are not seen as things that remain in the world and have value in themselves. Rather, they are objects that are waiting to be used. We might see examples of this in coal mining or oil drilling, or in various pieces of equipment, such as airplanes. However, is this view of objects waiting to be used not also true of art and books? Heidegger might claim that in the technological world, there is no difference. These objects are just part of a vast business network in which books are commissioned by publishers who believe a certain subject will be attractive to an audience. A produced book is like a pile of coal, waiting to be sold. In the modern world, according to many thinkers, it makes little difference if one sells wine or coal or cars or art. It is all part of a complex commercial network in which each thing becomes a commodity.

The fact that we ask questions about the technological worldview certainly does not mean that we would want to surrender technology and the vast complex that is founded on it—or even that we could if we chose to do so. However, that consideration makes it even more essential that we explore this worldview. It is a defining aspect of our culture, and we should attempt to understand both its benefits and its costs. When we do, we can begin to draft a new orientation toward it, which means also a new orientation toward our world and toward ourselves. Until we have thought through some of the issues raised by the conditions of life in a technological world, we will remain mere products of this world rather than its inhabitants. We will be shaped by our jobs, by our environments, and by the transformation of our efforts into commodities, but we will remain unaware of just *how* we are shaped by them. Instead of understanding the ways in which we are formed by a particular culture, we will think of ourselves as experiencing inevitable aspects of what it is to be human. We will be unable to ask questions, see consequences, and weigh alternatives. It is one of the primary goals of the Touchstones Discussion Project to enable all of us to see more clearly the conditions of our own lives. When we do, we gain the perspective we need to act deliberately and responsibly as we create our future together.

Session Strategy Worksheet

1. **Goals.** Consider the strengths and weaknesses of previous discussions and the progress of your group as a whole. What would you like for the group to accomplish in your session? Are there specific problems that need to be addressed, or perhaps a new skill that needs to be developed, or an issue that should be examined? Taking into account the texts as well as the history and needs of your group, what do you think would be important for the group to consider about these texts? Why?

2. **Handouts.** Will you have everyone complete a handout? If so, on a separate sheet, compose the handout that you will present. Will the participants complete the handout during the session, or do you need to distribute it before the session so that the participants can complete it in advance? Will you reserve any time in the session for a discussion of the handout? Will that time come before or after the general discussion?

3. **Small Group Work.** Will you have any small group work? If so, what will you have the groups do? Should the small group work come before or after the general discussion? Will you have the small groups report results to the larger group?

4. **Large Group Discussion.** How will you start the general discussion? Will you ask an opening question? Will you ask everyone to prepare and present an opening question? Or will you plan to move naturally from the reports of the small groups or consideration of the handout into the discussion? If you plan to ask an opening question, what will it be?

5. **Troubleshooting.** What problems do you anticipate may arise in the discussion of these texts? How might you plan to address such problems?

6. **Evaluations.** Will you have the participants fill out an evaluation sheet as part of the session? Will you reserve any part of the session for the group members to talk about the strengths and weaknesses of the session and discussion?

Four Who Mastered Science
A Tale from India

Long ago, a king ruled in the City of Flowers. In his kingdom, there were many members of the group called Brahmins. In one of the Brahmin colonies lived a man named Visnusvamin. This Brahmin and his wife lived happily together for many years and had four sons. When these sons became men, their parents died and left them a large inheritance. However, they had no guardian and adviser, so their relatives wasted and stole the brothers' money, and the young men became poor.

One day, they met together and decided that they had no future in that country. One of them suggested, "Why don't we go to the village where our grandfather lives? Look what our fate has brought us in our home. We have nothing here, and it can't be worse there." The other brothers agreed, and they set out on their journey. They had to beg their food as they made their way to their destination. Their maternal grandfather had died, but the brothers were received by their cousins. They lived with their cousins, had their meals there, and pursued their studies. At first, everything was fine, but soon they noticed that when food, clothes, and places to sleep were distributed, their portions became less and less. Their cousins' contempt worried the four brothers, and they met secretly to discuss the situation.

The oldest brother spoke first. "Brothers, what can a man do? Fate does everything, and we are powerless to change it. Today I was wandering around miserably when I came upon a funeral pyre. There I saw a corpse laid out on the ground waiting to be burned. As I looked at the sight of the dead body, I thought to myself, 'What a fortunate man. He is rid of his burden of sorrow and now he can take his rest.' So then and there I decided to end my life. I tied a rope to a tree and hanged myself. However, while I was unconscious but before my spirit departed, the rope was cut and I fell to the ground. When I opened my eyes, I found a man kneeling over me and waving his clothing about me to give me air and relief. 'Tell me, friend,' said the man. 'You are a man of learning. Why do you despair and try to do away with yourself? If you are wretched and unhappy, just get yourself to do good. Your spirit will become good, and your luck will change. Do you really want to exchange your present misery for the eternal suffering that is yours if you kill yourself?'"

One of the other brothers spoke next. "I agree that our lives are miserable. We are poor and have nothing. Fate has ruled us so that you couldn't even end your life. Why should we let fate rule us? We seek the wrong things if we hope for wealth and good fortune. Wealth is as changeable as the autumn clouds. Fortune is like a false friend or an unloving wife. We may win and hold them for a while, but they will never remain faithful. An intelligent man doesn't act this way. He masters a specialty, a science. This mastery will help him win back his money or his woman with his own brains as often as necessary."

At these words the oldest brother brightened up. "What specialty should we master?" he asked. They all began to think, and, coming up with no answer, they said, "Let us each search the earth, and learn a special science." So they agreed on a time and place to meet again, and each of the four brothers started off on his quest in a different direction.

Time passed, and the brothers returned to the meeting place. Each was excited to hear what the other had learned.

"I have mastered a science," said the youngest, "which enables me, if I have just one bone of an animal, to create the flesh that goes with it."

"And I," said the second, "know a science that will grow that creature's skin and hair, if I have a bone with flesh."

"And I," joined in the third, "have the knowledge to create its legs, head, and body, if I have the skin, flesh, and bone of a part."

"And I," hurriedly added the fourth, "have also mastered a science. If a creature is whole in bones, flesh and skin, I know how to give it life."

All the brothers were pleased at how their sciences fit together and at all the prospects the future now held for them. They rushed out to the jungle to find a piece of bone to demonstrate what they could do. Not long after they entered the jungle, they found a small bone. None of them could recognize the bone, and they hesitated. But then one asked, "Come, is all this science to become useless in our hands?" And they went to work. The first added the flesh, the second used his science to grow skin and hair, and the third completed the creature with limbs, a body, and a head. The four brothers approached the still unmoving creature, and the fourth gave the lion life. The ferocious beast immediately shook its heavy mane, bared its sharp teeth and merciless claws, and attacked its creators. It killed them and vanished into the depths of the jungle.

The four Brahmins perished because of their creation of a lion. And who can stay happy, if he makes something evil? So it may well happen that even a science that has cost a great deal of effort to learn may not work out to one's advantage. If fate is hostile, doom will come. Only if the roots of the tree of human effort are watered with intelligence and surrounded with a trench of worldly wisdom will the tree bear fruit.

The Question Concerning Technology
by Martin Heidegger

People say that modern technology is something entirely different from all earlier technologies. They say this because modern technology is based on modern physics, which is an exact science. However, we have realized that the reverse is also true. Modern physics uses experiments, and this is dependent on how well modern technology can produce the machines and equipment for experimentation. So, there is a mutual relationship between modern technology and modern physics. But this is just a historical fact. It tells us nothing about why there is such a relationship. The crucial question remains. What is modern technology like that it puts exact science to use?

What is modern technology? Like earlier types of technology, it is a way of revealing the things that are in the world. Only when our attention rests on this fundamental fact does what is truly new in modern technology show itself to us.

The way modern technology reveals what things in the world are like is not similar to earlier forms of technology and production. It is not like the way handcrafts, poetry, and art reveal things. They bring forward things in the world so we can see them in a new light. The way modern technology reveals the world to us is by challenging nature. It challenges nature with the unreasonable demand that nature supply energy which can be extracted, and then stored for later use. But isn't this also true of the old windmill? No! The windmill's sails do indeed turn in the wind, but it turns only when the wind is blowing. The windmill does not unlock energy from the air currents in order to store it.

In contrast, technology challenges a tract of land when it removes coal and ore. Technology then reveals the earth to us in a new way. The earth becomes a mining district. The soil becomes a mineral deposit. The field that the peasant used to cultivate and keep in order now appears very different from how it used to appear. In former times, "to keep in order" meant to take care of the field and to maintain it. The peasant never challenged the soil. When he sowed the grain, he placed the seed in the keeping of the forces of growth, and watched over and cared for it. But now, even the modern cultivation of a field is ruled by another kind of ordering. This new ordering sets upon nature and challenges it. Agriculture no longer involves the peasant caring for the field, but has become the mechanized food industry. With modern technology, the air is forced to surrender its nitrogen, the earth must yield up its ore, and this ore is further forced to give up its uranium, among other elements. But then uranium, in turn, is attacked to force out atomic energy, which can be released for destructive or peaceful uses.

Technology sets upon nature, and challenges it for energy. It unlocks what is in nature and exposes it. This unlocking and exposing is always for the purpose of yet something else. For example, to get maximum yield at minimum expense, coal hauled out of a mining district is not produced to be simply viewed or used. Instead, it is produced to be stored. It stays somewhere, just waiting to be called on to deliver up its energy. The coal is challenged to give up as steam the sun's warmth stored in it. This, later, is made to turn wheels to keep a factory going. And the sequence never ends. Modern technology reveals the things in the world in a particular way that comes from the way it approaches everything. It sets upon things and challenges them. Modern technology unlocks the energy that is hidden and concealed in nature. It not only brings out into the open what was hidden, but changes and transforms it. What is transformed is then merely stored up, and later distributed. The distribution goes from place to place, switching what it stored up through a network. This unlocking, transforming, storing up, distributing, and switching that technology applies to things that appear to us, determines how we view things. The whole procedure never comes to an end nor does it simply peter out. The way things are revealed is through the interlocking network through which they move in unending regulated ways. The regulation of the movement is everywhere made secure. Regulation and security even become the chief characteristics of modern technology, which reveals things by setting a challenge to them.

What particular kind of revealing is this? Everywhere, everything is ordered to stand by, indeed to stand there just waiting to be ordered again. This is a very special way of standing. We call it standing-reserve or just standing and waiting, waiting for another order. This phrase expresses something essential, and we miss it if we use the expression "stockpile." Modern technology reveals things to us as what stands in reserve and waits. The things in our world are no longer things. They are all standing and waiting to become something else. But isn't the airplane on the runway a thing? Yes, we can picture the machine in that way. But when we do, what this machine really is becomes hidden. Revealed as what it really is as an instrument, the airplane stands on the taxi strip and waits. It is ordered there to ensure the possibility of transportation. Both the whole structure of the airplane and every one of its parts is nothing at all but what waits on call for duty. It stands waiting for takeoff to somewhere else.

Discussion Evaluation Form

The items below are discussion dynamics that may or may not be present in your group. Decide to what extent you think that each dynamic was present in the discussion. Then decide whether you think the group needs to work to improve in this area.

	None Some Great deal	Need to Improve?
Dominance by some individuals	1 2 3 4 5 6 7 8 9 10	Yes ❏ No ❏
Cooperation	1 2 3 4 5 6 7 8 9 10	Yes ❏ No ❏
Silence	1 2 3 4 5 6 7 8 9 10	Yes ❏ No ❏
Interrupting	1 2 3 4 5 6 7 8 9 10	Yes ❏ No ❏
Respect	1 2 3 4 5 6 7 8 9 10	Yes ❏ No ❏
Balanced participation	1 2 3 4 5 6 7 8 9 10	Yes ❏ No ❏
Active listening	1 2 3 4 5 6 7 8 9 10	Yes ❏ No ❏
Lack of interest	1 2 3 4 5 6 7 8 9 10	Yes ❏ No ❏
Asking one other questions	1 2 3 4 5 6 7 8 9 10	Yes ❏ No ❏
Building on one other's contributions	1 2 3 4 5 6 7 8 9 10	Yes ❏ No ❏
Many people talking at once	1 2 3 4 5 6 7 8 9 10	Yes ❏ No ❏

Pick one of the dynamics that you think the group should work to improve, and explain why.

How would you rate this discussion on a scale of 1–10? _____

Strategy Evaluation Worksheet

1. How would you rate the discussion on a scale of 1 to 10, with 1 being least successful and 10 being most successful? Why?

2. What did the leaders do that differed from your strategy for this session?

3. What was the opening question? Do you think it was a good question? Why or why not?

4. What topics were not raised that you thought should have been?

5. Are there things the leaders did not do that you think they should have?

6. Are there things the leaders did do that you think they should not have?

19

Community and the Individual

In Unit 17, we considered the tension between our experience as individuals and as members of a group by looking at ways in which our individuality can be effaced or absorbed by the group. In this meeting, you may want to consider this tension from the other side—by looking at the responsibilities we have toward the community. There are many approaches one could take to this consideration. The texts by Benedict de Spinoza and Mao Tse Tung take up the issue by asking how much control society should have over our thought. Another approach—one that sets the stage for the question that the texts' authors pose—would be to inquire about the nature of the individual prior to the community, and then ask how our nature must change in order for us to become part of a community. Are there aspects of ourselves that we must give up to enter into society? Are there parts of who we are that can *only* be realized in relationship with others? Many writers have theorized about this question by imagining what we would be like in a state of nature, a place before or outside society, and then thinking through the changes that life within a society imposes on us.

Thomas Hobbes, John Locke, and Jean Jacques Rousseau—the political theorists of the seventeenth and eighteenth centuries to whom we largely owe our modern understanding of the nature of the state—all used this method to refine their theories. Each of their writings presents a definite view of how we would be prior to membership in a society, how we enter society, and what we are like within it. Hobbes holds that in the state of nature, we are essentially competitive, selfish, and desiring creatures. We move into society to ensure our security and are kept in order by fear—but our natures never really change. Locke, the thinker on whom the founders of the United States most explicitly relied, argues that people are already rational prior to society and able to legitimately claim ownership of some things. He agrees with Hobbes, however, that individuals remain the same persons when they enter society that they were outside it. One of the most important differences between the two thinkers occurs on the very question we are considering, that of our responsibility to the society. Hobbes conceives our responsibility to any society that preserves us from a state of anarchy as being total; we are all in a state of contractual obligation to the state, which conversely has no meaningful obligation toward the individual. For Locke, although we have certain responsibilities toward society, society also has important responsibilities toward us, especially the responsibility to protect our property. Rousseau's perspective is, in some ways, a hybrid of the two. Like Hobbes, he claims that in a state of nature, we are essentially competitive and slaves to our desires. However, entry into society transforms us from animals to human beings—to creatures capable of the real freedom that comes from acting by reason instead of by impulse. On the question of our obligation to society, his reasoning is very complex. We enter society through a social contract and thus become rational. In that we are rational, our ends and those of the society should be in agreement. Yet sometimes we may still act from our individual desires. In these cases, the society must force us to be reasonable— essentially, force us to be free. This means that we have a duty to the society to be rational, and it, through its laws, can make us act in a rational way. Rousseau's theory can become the basis for our having a complete duty to a society that had formed us as rational beings and that we ourselves have formed through the social contract.

In contrast to the thinkers we have mentioned, other philosophers have held that what we have been calling the state of nature is really inconceivable. From their point of view, we as people and individuals can only exist within a society. An important proponent of such a view is Aristotle. He believed that we are by our nature social or political animals. There is simply no human nature outside society. A person existing outside a community is or becomes either a god or a wild beast. From this point of view, of course, speculation about any supposed state of nature is both misguided and pointless; the view holds that only within a society are we capable of investigating what we truly are.

It is important to remember that, even for those who speculated about it, the state of nature was not meant to refer to a real time in our historical past. It functioned rather as an exploratory device. In using it, political theorists were asking a question that might be considered analogous to the question of how we appear when examined though the discipline of psychology rather than through that of sociology. Aristotle's position is somewhat like claiming that sociology comes prior to psychology—that we develop a mind and become a subject for psychology to study only within a society. Recent trends in the study of animal behavior would seem to support Aristotle's approach; observing an animal in isolation in a laboratory or zoo seems to tell us remarkably little about what that animal is like in its usual social environment and habitat.

In considering this unit's passages by Spinoza and Mao, it is useful to consider how much of what we would call ourselves is given to us only by our participation in society and to what extent it makes sense to think of the individual outside any society. The selection by Spinoza asks whether the state should attempt to control not only what people do but also what they think and say. He concludes that although a state must control actions, to attempt to control thought would be foolish. You might consider the question of whether a government should control speech. Is speech simply an expression of thought, or is it a form of action? Spinoza's position eventually became the basis of freedom of speech as it is protected in the U.S. Constitution. But should all speech be protected? For instance, is commercial advertising speech that should be protected? In addition, the group might consider whether our freedom of speech gives us an actual responsibility to announce our disagreements with our country's policies—in other words, to engage in opposition by speech rather than through the coups and uprisings that characterize so many societies.

The second text comes from a very different perspective. For Mao, all thought and writing and all speech and art are enmeshed in the political and economic framework within which one lives. Artists and writers therefore have a social and political responsibility. One cannot be neutral in one's thought and speech because whatever one says or thinks is an expression of one's class position. One implication of Mao's position is that any person who, unlike Mao, advocates free speech, imagines that thought and speech are somehow not fully determined by political and social factors—that we can somehow think and speak from a position "outside" our social location. But to what extent is this genuinely possible? Should we feel that we are responsible to our community for what we say and think, or are we free from that responsibility when we remain at the level of thought and speech?

During the previous sessions, you also have been creating a community. Although you didn't enter it from a state of nature, you did come from one sort of social and even political relationship with one another to create a different one. It would be useful to reflect on the changes that have occurred in this microsociety and whether any of these can be extrapolated to other organizations or parts of our lives. We came into the discussion group with many ideas about what we desired as individuals, how we would relate to others in the group, and what we expected from the group. It would be interesting to examine these initial expectations and attitudes and whether they changed as the group formed into a community capable of exploring and examining new ideas, concepts, and ways of behaving toward one another.

Session Strategy Worksheet

1. **Goals.** Consider the strengths and weaknesses of previous discussions and the progress of your group as a whole. What would you like for the group to accomplish in your session? Are there specific problems that need to be addressed, or perhaps a new skill that needs to be developed, or an issue that should be examined? Taking into account the texts as well as the history and needs of your group, what do you think would be important for the group to consider about these texts? Why?

2. **Handouts.** Will you have everyone complete a handout? If so, on a separate sheet, compose the handout that you will present. Will the participants complete the handout during the session, or do you need to distribute it before the session so that the participants can complete it in advance? Will you reserve any time in the session for a discussion of the handout? Will that time come before or after the general discussion?

3. **Small Group Work.** Will you have any small group work? If so, what will you have the groups do? Should the small group work come before or after the general discussion? Will you have the small groups report results to the larger group?

4. **Large Group Discussion.** How will you start the general discussion? Will you ask an opening question? Will you ask everyone to prepare and present an opening question? Or will you plan to move naturally from the reports of the small groups or consideration of the handout into the discussion? If you plan to ask an opening question, what will it be?

5. **Troubleshooting.** What problems do you anticipate may arise in the discussion of these texts? How might you plan to address such problems?

6. **Evaluations.** Will you have the participants fill out an evaluation sheet as part of the session? Will you reserve any part of the session for the group members to talk about the strengths and weaknesses of the session and discussion?

The Theologico-Political Treatise
by Benedict de Spinoza

If men's minds were as easily controlled as their tongues, every king would sit safely on his throne. Governments would not have to compel their subjects. Subjects would agree with their ruler's decision that something was true or false, good or evil, just or unjust. However, no man's mind can possibly be wholly at another's command. No one can willingly transfer his natural right of free reason and judgment. Nor can anyone be compelled to do it. Therefore, any government that attempts to control minds is considered tyrannical. It is held to be an abuse of sovereignty and a violation of the rights of subjects when a government seeks to command what shall be accepted as true or rejected as false, or what opinions men should hold about God. All these questions fall within a man's natural right that he cannot give up even if he wishes to do so.

However unlimited a sovereign's power may be, or however much the rulers are trusted as spokesmen of law and religion, the government can never prevent men from forming judgments and being influenced by their feelings. The government, indeed, certainly has the right to treat as enemies all men whose opinions, on all matters, disagree with its own. But we are not here discussing its strict rights but rather its proper course of action. I grant that government has the right to rule in the most violent manner. It can put citizens to death for the most trivial causes, but no one can imagine that it would be very sensible to do this. In fact, insofar as such action would cause extreme peril to itself, we may even deny that it has the power to act violently or, consequently, even the absolute right to act in this way. For the rights of a sovereign are matters of judgment. But every man is, by natural right, master of his own thoughts. It follows that men, thinking in different and contradictory ways, cannot, without disastrous results, be forced to speak only the opinions and views of the government. In addition, even the most experienced men, to say nothing of the multitude, do not know how to keep silent. Everyone's common failing is to confide his plans to others even when there is a need for secrecy. So a government would be extremely harsh if it deprived the individual of his freedom of saying and teaching what he thought. It would be moderate if it granted such freedom. Still, we can't deny that the authority of a government can be as much injured by words as by actions. Therefore, though the freedom we are discussing cannot entirely be denied to subjects, its unlimited presence would be most harmful. We must inquire how far such freedom can be granted without danger to the peace of the state or the power of the rulers.

The ultimate aim of government is not to rule by fear or to exact obedience. Instead, a government's aim is to free every man from fear so that he may live as securely as possible. In other words, the aim is to increase man's natural right to exist and work without injuring himself or others. The object of government is not to change men from rational beings into animals or puppets. It is to enable men to develop their minds and bodies in security, and to employ their reason. The true aim of government is liberty.

In a state, the power of making laws must either rest with all the citizens, with some of them, or in one man. Since the judgments men make differ greatly from one another, and since each man thinks he alone knows everything, it is necessary that individuals surrender their right of acting entirely on their own judgment in order to preserve peace. The individual citizen thus gives up his right of free action though his reason and judgment remain free. No one can act against the authorities without danger to the state. However, his feelings and opinions may be at odds with the state. Therefore, the government should allow any man to speak from a rational conviction and not from anger, hatred, or fraud, and provided he doesn't try, on his own, to introduce any change in the state.

So, from these considerations, we can recognize which opinions the state should forbid. The state can suppress those opinions that by their nature nullify and deny the agreement by which men give up the freedom to act as they wish when they formed the state. However, even this case is not so much a matter of opinions, as these opinions are themselves actions. For whoever maintains such theories nullifies the contract that he implicitly or explicitly made with his rulers. Such opinions may therefore be suppressed, but others that do not violate the contract that formed the state may not.

Freedom may indeed be crushed, and men may be so bound down that they don't dare whisper anything except at the command of their rulers. But this can never be carried so far as to make them think according to the wishes of that authority. So, the necessary consequence would be that men would be daily thinking one thing and saying another. This would corrupt good faith, which is the main support of government. It would also encourage flattery and dishonesty from which spring plots of all kinds and lead to the destruction of everything good.

The Yenan Forum on Art and Literature
by Mao Tse Tung

All art, literature, and thought represent the interests of some class in society. Indeed, there exist literature and art that are for the exploiters and oppressors. Feudal literature and art are literature and art of the ruling class in China's feudal era. To this day, such literature and art still have considerable influence in China. Literature and art for the middle class, the bourgeoisie, are bourgeois literature and art. With us, literature and art are for the people, not for any of the above groups. We have said that China's new culture at the present stage is an anti-imperialist, anti-feudal culture of the masses of the people under the leadership of the proletariat. Today, anything that is truly of the masses must necessarily be led by the most advanced workers. Whatever is under the leadership of the middle class property owner, the bourgeoisie, cannot possibly be for the masses. Naturally, the same applies to the new literature and art that are part of our new culture.

Who then, are the masses of the people? The greatest portion of the people, constituting more than 90 percent of our total population, are the factory workers, farm laborers, peasants, soldiers, and owners of small businesses. Therefore, our literature and art are first for the workers, the class that leads the revolution. Second, they are for the farm laborers and peasants, the most numerous and most steadfast of our allies in the revolution.

Our literary and art workers must alter their viewpoint. They must give up the idea that art and thought go beyond and are outside of political concerns. They must gradually move their feet over to the side of the workers, peasants, and soldiers, to the side of the proletariat, through the process of going into their very midst and into the thick of practical struggles, and through the process of studying Marxism and society. Only in this way can we have a literature and art that are truly for the workers, peasants, and soldiers, a truly proletarian literature and art.

Man's social life is the only source of literature and art and is itself incomparably livelier and richer in content. But the people are not satisfied with life alone and demand literature and art as well. Why? Because, while both are beautiful, life as reflected in works of literature and art can and ought to be on a higher plane, more intense, more concentrated, more typical, nearer the ideal, and therefore more universal than actual everyday life. Revolutionary literature and art should create a variety of characters out of real life, and help the masses to propel history forward. For example, there is suffering from hunger and cold on the one hand, and exploitation and oppression of man by man on the other. These facts exist everywhere and people look upon them as commonplace. Writers and artists concentrate and intensify such everyday facts, typify the contradictions and struggles within them, and produce works that awaken the masses. These works fire the masses with enthusiasm and impel them to unite and struggle to transform their environment. Without such literature and art, our political and social task could not be fulfilled, or at least not so effectively and speedily. Through the creative labor of revolutionary writers and artists, the raw materials found in the life of the people are shaped into the ideological form of literature and art serving the masses of the people. All our literature and art, whether more advanced or elementary, exist for the masses of the people. All our works of art are created for the workers, peasants, and soldiers and are for their use.

A poem, novel, and painting is good only when it brings real benefit to the masses of the people. Your work may be as beautiful a poem as "The Spring Snow," but if for the time being it appeals only to the few and the masses are still singing crude works like the "Song of the Rural Poor," you will get nowhere by simply scolding them. Instead, you must work to raise their level of understanding and enjoyment. The question now is to bring about a unity between "The Spring Snow" and the "Song of the Rural Poor," between higher standards and popularization. Without such a unity, the highest art of any artist cannot help being simply for the political and social use of a small, self-interested group. You may call this art "pure and lofty," but that is merely your own name for it that the masses will not accept.

Discussion Evaluation Form

The items below are discussion dynamics that may or may not be present in your group. Decide to what extent you think that each dynamic was present in the discussion. Then decide whether you think the group needs to work to improve in this area.

	None Some Great deal	Need to Improve?
Dominance by some individuals	1 2 3 4 5 6 7 8 9 10	Yes ❑ No ❑
Cooperation	1 2 3 4 5 6 7 8 9 10	Yes ❑ No ❑
Silence	1 2 3 4 5 6 7 8 9 10	Yes ❑ No ❑
Interrupting	1 2 3 4 5 6 7 8 9 10	Yes ❑ No ❑
Respect	1 2 3 4 5 6 7 8 9 10	Yes ❑ No ❑
Balanced participation	1 2 3 4 5 6 7 8 9 10	Yes ❑ No ❑
Active listening	1 2 3 4 5 6 7 8 9 10	Yes ❑ No ❑
Lack of interest	1 2 3 4 5 6 7 8 9 10	Yes ❑ No ❑
Asking one other questions	1 2 3 4 5 6 7 8 9 10	Yes ❑ No ❑
Building on one other's contributions	1 2 3 4 5 6 7 8 9 10	Yes ❑ No ❑
Many people talking at once	1 2 3 4 5 6 7 8 9 10	Yes ❑ No ❑

Pick one of the dynamics that you think the group should work to improve, and explain why.

How would you rate this discussion on a scale of 1–10? _____

Strategy Evaluation Worksheet

1. How would you rate the discussion on a scale of 1 to 10, with 1 being least successful and 10 being most successful? Why?

2. What did the leaders do that differed from your strategy for this session?

3. What was the opening question? Do you think it was a good question? Why or why not?

4. What topics were not raised that you thought should have been?

5. Are there things the leaders did not do that you think they should have?

6. Are there things the leaders did do that you think they should not have?

Perspectives on the World

Mapping the Future was designed to enable a collection of individuals to develop the skills and discernment necessary for forming a group that explores significant questions together. As our world becomes increasingly complex and our problems increasingly interdependent, we are moving from a situation in which thought is largely the solitary activity depicted in Rodin's sculpture *The Thinker*, which represents a lone man in a deep state of concentration, to a situation in which thought must be more and more a cooperative effort. The perspectives and talents of each of us are essential as we work together to find new ways of thinking and engaging with one another—new ways of being in this world that we together both create and inhabit.

In *Mapping the Future*, we have attempted to reach these goals by using a set of texts and the process of discussion to examine our presuppositions and fundamental opinions. If we are able to see and examine these, then we can both orient ourselves with respect to them and consider whether and how we might change them. Such awareness also sets the stage for further explorations, either together with this group or in other circumstances. The skills that you have been developing, although they are unusual and gained only through strenuous effort, do not isolate you from others. Rather, they give you the ability to build bridges and reach out to those around you. As you move through the world, you will be a resource to any group you enter. You have been practicing the art of discussion and can share that with others.

Our method for locating and orienting ourselves has involved a sort of triangulation using texts, our responses to them, and reflection on the process of creating a discussion group as the three points of the triangle. In the introduction to this book, we described the multiple perspectives on ourselves that we hoped to achieve by comparing the paired texts both with each other and with our own perspectives. Any single perspective could have given us an important view of an issue or attitude that we need to examine as we come to know ourselves and our emerging world. However, each particular point of view is also limited by the very perspective it presents. We see this limitation all the time with maps. Mapmakers must use a variety of methods to represent the same bodies of water and land. The challenge is to present or project the three-dimensional world onto a two-dimensional surface. The two most prevalent ways of doing this are called Mercator and polar projections. In a Mercator projection, the resulting map is most accurate at the equator and least accurate at the poles. Remember how gigantic Greenland appears on the maps that hang on classroom walls? To balance this distortion, mapmakers can use a polar projection, which is accurate at the poles but distorts the area at the equator. To achieve an accurate picture, we need both of these maps as well as others that give us yet additional perspectives.

The texts for this session present very intriguing examples of multiple perspectives and of the complex understanding of our situation that such perspectives can allow us to achieve. There is perhaps no other work in our culture that demands some response from each of us as insistently as does the opening of Genesis. Almost everyone is at least somewhat familiar with it, and to some measure accepts or rejects its claims. The ubiquity of this story means that our neutrality is close to impossible; whether we consider the text to be literature, myth, or a straightforward account of historical events, or even if we dismiss it, we are already taking an attitude toward it. Biblical scholars often propose that the differing accounts of creation in the first and second chapters of Genesis are from different traditions or authors. Regardless of whether this hypothesis is correct, at whatever moment it was that Genesis emerged as the text we have today, it was decided that both narratives were necessary. As a group, reflect on the differences between the two chapters and consider why the decision might have been made to include both in a single document—a foundational document for a people. What does it mean that we seem to have two perspectives present from the very beginning of this story that we tell about ourselves? Do the stories contradict one another? Or does one perhaps further the other or present the same story from a different angle? What might our sense of the world or of creation be if we had only one of these accounts? How do the two stories work together to shape our understanding of creation? The ability to openly explore and speculate about these texts, working together with others to discover what they can reveal to us about ourselves and our world rather than attempting to convince or convert, is a considerable accomplishment. Doing so can give us a sense of renewed possibilities, not only for ourselves but for the world we share.

The use of paired texts has not been the only way in which an interest in multiple perspectives has characterized our work together. We have frequently said that one goal in forming a discussion group is for each member to view herself or himself simultaneously as a leader and as a participant. This is an important part of what it means to genuinely work together as co-explorers and co-creators. *Mapping the Future* is an experiment in shared leadership. Now, as you have reached the end of this adventure together, you should spend some time reflecting on your journey. What sort of story would you tell about what has happened over the course of the program? How has your group changed over time? How has your perspective evolved? What were the hardest goals for you all to reach? Were there decisive sessions for the development of your group—moments when you leapt ahead or when you despaired of making any progress at all? If you were writing a story of your group, what perspectives would you want to take into account? You might try preparing a short story of a paragraph or so in length to compare with the accounts of the other group members. Examining the ways in which your accounts converge or conflict as well as examining the differences of emphasis and the similarities of approach might help you see even more clearly the terrain that you have mapped together and the directions you might take as you move into the future.

Session Strategy Worksheet

1. **Goals.** Consider the strengths and weaknesses of previous discussions and the progress of your group as a whole. What would you like for the group to accomplish in your session? Are there specific problems that need to be addressed, or perhaps a new skill that needs to be developed, or an issue that should be examined? Taking into account the texts as well as the history and needs of your group, what do you think would be important for the group to consider about these texts? Why?

2. **Handouts.** Will you have everyone complete a handout? If so, on a separate sheet, compose the handout that you will present. Will the participants complete the handout during the session, or do you need to distribute it before the session so that the participants can complete it in advance? Will you reserve any time in the session for a discussion of the handout? Will that time come before or after the general discussion?

3. **Small Group Work.** Will you have any small group work? If so, what will you have the groups do? Should the small group work come before or after the general discussion? Will you have the small groups report results to the larger group?

4. **Large Group Discussion.** How will you start the general discussion? Will you ask an opening question? Will you ask everyone to prepare and present an opening question? Or will you plan to move naturally from the reports of the small groups or consideration of the handout into the discussion? If you plan to ask an opening question, what will it be?

5. **Troubleshooting.** What problems do you anticipate may arise in the discussion of these texts? How might you plan to address such problems?

6. **Evaluations.** Will you have the participants fill out an evaluation sheet as part of the session? Will you reserve any part of the session for the group members to talk about the strengths and weaknesses of the session and discussion?

Genesis 1:1–2:3
from the Bible

In the beginning God created the heavens and the earth. Now the earth was empty, shapeless, and dark. God's spirit moved over the water.

God said, "Let there be light." And there was light. God saw that the light was good, and divided the light from the darkness. God called the light "day," and the darkness he called "night." This was the morning and evening of the first day.

God said, "Let there be a dome to divide the waters in two." God made the dome, and it divided the water above from the waters below. God called this dome "heaven." This was the morning and evening of the second day.

God said, "Let the waters under heaven come together, and let dry land appear." And so it happened. God called the dry land "earth," and the waters he called "sea." God saw that this was good.

God said, "Let the earth produce vegetation; seed-bearing plants and fruit trees." And so it happened. The earth produced vegetation: plants of all kinds bearing seed, and trees of all kinds bearing fruit. God saw that this was good. This was the morning and evening of the third day.

God said, "Let there be lights in the heaven to divide day from night, and let them show the passage of time, that is, of days and years, and of holidays. Let these lights in the heaven shine on earth." And so it happened. God made two great lights, the greater light to govern the day, and the smaller to govern the night, and He also made the stars. God set these lights in the heaven to shine on earth, to govern the day and night, and to divide light from darkness. God saw that this was good. This was the morning and evening of the fourth day.

God said, "Let the waters be filled with living creatures, and let birds fly above the earth within the dome of the heavens." And so it happened. God created whales and fish, and all the kinds of birds and said, "Be fruitful and multiply, and fill the waters of the seas; and let the birds multiply upon the earth." This was the morning and evening of the fifth day.

God said, "Let the earth produce all the kinds of living creatures: tame animals, wild animals, and all the animals that crawl." And so it happened. God made every kind of wild animal, every kind of tame animal, and every kind of animal that crawls. God saw that this was good.

God said, "Let us make man in our own image, so that they are like ourselves, and let them be masters of the fish of the sea, the birds of heaven, the tame animals, the wild animals, and all the animals that crawl upon the earth." God created man in the image of Himself, in the image of God. He created male and female.

God blessed them, saying to them, "Be fruitful, multiply, fill the earth, and conquer it. Be masters of the fish of the sea, birds of the air, and all living animals upon the earth." God said, "See, I give you all the seed-bearing plants and all the trees with fruit; this shall be your food. To all the wild animals, birds of heaven, and animals that crawl upon the earth, I give the

MAPPING THE FUTURE

grass and leaves of plants as food." And so it happened. God saw all He had made, and indeed it was very good. This was the morning and evening of the sixth day.

Thus the heaven and the earth were completed. On the seventh day God completed the work He had been doing. He rested on the seventh day after his work. God blessed the seventh day and made it holy, because on that day, He rested after his work of creating. This is how the heaven and earth were created.

Genesis 2:4–3:24

from the Bible

When God made heaven and earth, there were neither wild bushes on the earth nor had any plants sprung up. This was because God hadn't sent rain onto the earth, nor was there any man to till the ground. Instead, water would rise up from out of the ground, and flood the surface. God formed man out of the dust of the soil. He breathed the breath of life into man's nostrils and thus man became a living creature.

Then God planted a garden in Eden, which is to the east, and there He put the man whom He had made. God made trees spring up from the ground. The garden contained all the trees that were pleasing to see and good to eat. And in the middle of the garden, He placed the tree of life and the tree of the knowledge of good and evil. A river flowing from Eden watered the garden, and, when it left the garden split into four streams named Pishon, Gihon, Tigris, and Euphrates. God took the man He had made and placed him in the garden to till the soil and care for it. Then God gave man this warning: "You may eat the fruit from all the trees in the garden except one. You must not eat the fruit from the tree of the knowledge of good and evil. For on the day that you eat of that tree, you will certainly die."

God said, "It isn't good for man to be alone. I will make him a companion and partner." So God took the soil and made all the wild animals and all the birds of heaven. He then brought the animals and birds to Adam to see what he would call them. Thus, each animal and each bird would be called by the name the man gave them. The man named all the cattle, all the birds of heaven, and all the wild beasts. But he did not find any animal that would be a suitable companion for him. So God put man into a very deep sleep. While he slept, God took one of the man's ribs and enclosed it in flesh. He made this rib into a woman and brought her to the man. The man said, "At last! This is bone from my bones and flesh from my flesh. She shall be called woman because she was taken from man."

This is why today a man leaves his father and mother and joins himself to his wife, and the two become one flesh.

The man and his wife in the garden were both naked, but they felt no shame toward one another. Of all the wild beasts God had made, the serpent was the craftiest and most cunning. He approached the woman and asked, "Did God really tell you not to eat the fruit from any of the trees in the garden?" The woman answered the serpent, "We may eat the fruit of all the trees in the garden except for the tree in the middle. About the fruit of that tree God said, 'You must not eat it or touch it. If you do, you shall die!'" The serpent said to the woman, "You won't die! God knows that the moment you eat the fruit of that tree, your eyes will be opened. You will be like gods, knowing both good and evil." The woman saw that the fruit of the tree was good to eat and pleasing to look at. And it was desirable because of the knowledge it could give. So she took some of the fruit and ate it. Then she gave some to her husband and he ate it. At that moment their eyes were opened and they realized they were naked. So they sewed fig leaves together to make themselves loincloths to wear.

In the evening, the man and woman heard God walking in the garden, and they hid from Him among the trees. God called out to the man, "Where are you?"

The man replied, "I heard the sound of your walking in the garden, and I was frightened because I was naked. So I hid myself."

"Who told you that you were naked?" God asked. "Have you been eating the fruit of the tree in the middle of the garden, which I told you never to eat?"

"It was the fault of the woman you gave me," the man said. "She gave me the fruit and I ate it."

Then God asked the woman, "What have you done?" The woman answered, "The serpent tricked me and I ate."

God spoke to the serpent, "Because you did this, you will be cursed more than all the cattle and all the wild beasts. From now on, you will crawl on your stomach and eat dust all the days of your life. You and the woman, your offspring and her offspring, will be enemies. Her offspring will strike at your head, and your offspring will strike at their feet."

To the woman, God said, "I will increase your pain in childbearing. In pain, you shall give birth to your children. You will yearn for your husband, and he will be your master."

Then God spoke to the man, "Because you listened to your wife and ate the fruit that I had forbidden you to eat, the soil will be cursed and you will get your food from it with suffering every day of your life. The ground will yield you thorns and thistles and there will be nothing but wild plants for you to eat. You will eat your bread with sweat still on your brow until you die, and you will return to the ground as you were taken from it. For dust you are, and to dust you will return."

The man named his wife Eve because she is the mother of all who live. God made clothes from skins for the man and his wife, and they began to wear them. Then God said, "The man has become like one of us, knowing good and evil. What if he takes fruit from the tree of life, eats it and lives forever?" So God drove them out of the Garden of Eden to till the soil from which He had originally made them. He drove them out. And to the east of Eden, He stationed angels and a flaming sword to guard the way to the tree of life, so they could never eat of it.

Discussion Evaluation Form

The items below are discussion dynamics that may or may not be present in your group. Decide to what extent you think that each dynamic was present in the discussion. Then decide whether you think the group needs to work to improve in this area.

	None Some Great deal	Need to Improve?
Dominance by some individuals	1 2 3 4 5 6 7 8 9 10	Yes ❑ No ❑
Cooperation	1 2 3 4 5 6 7 8 9 10	Yes ❑ No ❑
Silence	1 2 3 4 5 6 7 8 9 10	Yes ❑ No ❑
Interrupting	1 2 3 4 5 6 7 8 9 10	Yes ❑ No ❑
Respect	1 2 3 4 5 6 7 8 9 10	Yes ❑ No ❑
Balanced participation	1 2 3 4 5 6 7 8 9 10	Yes ❑ No ❑
Active listening	1 2 3 4 5 6 7 8 9 10	Yes ❑ No ❑
Lack of interest	1 2 3 4 5 6 7 8 9 10	Yes ❑ No ❑
Asking one other questions	1 2 3 4 5 6 7 8 9 10	Yes ❑ No ❑
Building on one other's contributions	1 2 3 4 5 6 7 8 9 10	Yes ❑ No ❑
Many people talking at once	1 2 3 4 5 6 7 8 9 10	Yes ❑ No ❑

Pick one of the dynamics that you think the group should work to improve, and explain why.

How would you rate this discussion on a scale of 1–10? _____

Strategy Evaluation Worksheet

1. How would you rate the discussion on a scale of 1 to 10, with 1 being least successful and 10 being most successful? Why?

2. What did the leaders do that differed from your strategy for this session?

3. What was the opening question? Do you think it was a good question? Why or why not?

4. What topics were not raised that you thought should have been?

5. Are there things the leaders did not do that you think they should have?

6. Are there things the leaders did do that you think they should not have?

Biographies

Aquinas, Saint Thomas (1225–74) was born at his father's castle Roccasecca, near Naples, Italy. From 1239–44, he attended the University of Naples, at the time one of the few universities at which a full range of Aristotelian doctrine was studied. Around 1250, he was ordained as a priest, and from 1252 to 1259, Aquinas taught at the Dominican House of Studies in Paris, where he was made a master of theology. In 1259, Aquinas returned to Naples to serve as a lector at Orvieto. He began writing his most significant work, *Summa Theologica*, in 1266. He died at the Cistercian Abbey of Fossanova on March 7, 1274.

Arendt, Hannah (1906–75) was born in Hanover, Germany. She was a political theorist who described "totalitarianism." Arendt studied under Martin Heidegger at the University of Heidelberg, where she received her doctorate at the age of 22. In 1933, she went to France to escape the Nazis and, in 1941, fled to the United States, becoming a U.S. citizen in 1951. Arendt served as research director for the Conference on Jewish Relations, executive secretary at the Jewish Cultural Reconstruction Organization, and visiting professor at Princeton and Columbia Universities. She also served as a professor at the University of Chicago, at University of California—Berkeley, and at the New School for Social Research. She wrote several books, including *Origins of Totalitarianism* (1951), *The Human Condition* (1958), *On Revolution* (1963), *Eichmann in Jerusalem* (1963), and *On Violence* (1970).

Augustine, Saint (354–430) was born in Thagaste, Numidia (now Suk Arras, Algeria). He was educated as a rhetorician in the former North African cities of Thagaste, Madaura, and Carthage. About 384, Augustine settled in Milan, Italy. There he came under the influence of the Neoplatonists and also met the bishop of Milan, Saint Ambrose. He was baptized by Ambrose on Easter Eve in 387. He returned to North Africa and was ordained in 391. In 395, he became bishop of Hippo (now Annaba, Algeria), an office he held until his death. It was during this time that Augustine developed his doctrines of original sin and divine grace, divine sovereignty, and predestination. He is best known for his autobiographical work *Confessions*, which related his early life and conversion. Other works include *The City of God* (413–26); his treatises "On Free Will" (388–95), "On Christian Doctrine" (397), "On Baptism: Against the Donatists" (400), "On the Trinity" (400–16), and "On Nature and Grace" (415); and homilies on several books of the Bible. Augustine died at Hippo on August 28, 430.

Bacon, Francis (1561–1626) was born in London, England. He entered Trinity College, Cambridge, in 1573. He studied law, became a barrister in 1582, and filled several public offices throughout his career, including the chancellorship. He was most known, however, for his endeavors to reorganize the natural sciences, which had an enormous impact on subsequent scientific inquiry. Most notable of Bacon's works is *Novum Organum* (1620). He died in 1626 and was buried at St. Michael's Church in Saint Albans. His final work, *The World*, came out three years after his death.

Camus, Albert (1913–60) was born in Mondovi, Algeria. He studied philosophy at the University of Algiers and worked as an actor, teacher, playwright, and journalist there and in Paris. Active in the French resistance during World War II, he became co-editor with Jean Paul Sartre of the left-wing newspaper *Combat* until 1948. He earned an international reputation with his novel *The Stranger* (1942). Later novels included *The Plague* (1947) and The Fall (1956). He also wrote plays and several political works. He received the Nobel Prize for Literature in 1957.

Collingwood, R. G. (1843–89) was born in Lancashire, England. He was educated at Oxford University, where he later became a professor of metaphysical philosophy. His work concentrated on the relationship between philosophy and history. He made notable contributions to the field of archaeology and was an authority on the history of Roman Britain. Collingwood was the author of several books in his lifetime, including *An Autobiography* (1939) and *Essay on Metaphysics* (1940). He was best known for two posthumously published works, T*he Idea of Nature* (1945) and *The Idea of History* (1946).

d'Hericourt, Jenny (1809–75) was born in Besançon, France, and she studied medicine privately in Paris and Chicago. She is known for her involvement in women's rights: she organized a society for women's civil liberties, helped to influence elections, and wrote *A Woman's Philosophy of Woman*. This book, published in 1860, influenced feminists in the United States, Italy, Russia, and France.

Douglass, Frederick (1817–95) was born Frederick Augustus Washington Bailey on the Eastern Shore of Maryland to a slave mother and a white father he never knew. In 1838, he escaped to New York City, where he changed his name to Frederick Douglass. He later moved to New Bedford, Massachusetts, where he met the prominent abolitionist William Lloyd Garrison. In 1841, Douglass became a lecturer for the American Anti-Slavery Society. In 1845, the society helped him publish his autobiography, *Narrative of the Life of Frederick Douglass, an American Slave*. In 1847, he launched his own newspaper, the *North Star*. After breaking with Garrison over ideological differences, Douglass continued to write and lecture on the injustices of slavery, becoming one of the most prominent voices of the movement. Douglass became the first black citizen to hold high rank (as U.S. minister and consul general to Haiti) in the U.S. government.

du Chatelet, Emilie (1706–49) was born in France in 1706 to a wealthy family. In 1739, she began to write a textbook for her son on Leibniz's physics. In 1740, she published this work, which she called *Institutions de physique*. It remains one of the clearest accounts of Leibnizian physics. However, Chatelet is best known for her work *Mathematical Principles of Natural Philosophy*, a French translation and analysis of Newton's *Principia*. Although she was not a creator of original mathematics, her work of translation, commentary, and synthesis contributed significantly to the development of Newtonian science in the middle eighteenth century in Europe because her book made Newton's work available to French mathematicians and scholars.

Ellison, Ralph (1914–94) was born in Oklahoma City, Oklahoma. In 1933, he left Oklahoma to study music at Tuskegee Institute in Alabama but soon became more focused on modern literature. In 1936, he moved to New York City, where he met Langston Hughes and Richard Wright. As a writer with the New Deal's Federal Writer's Project, Ellison produced many articles and essays concerning African American issues and culture. In 1945, he began writing *The Invisible Man*, which was published in 1953. Although a second book was rumored, Ellison never published another novel. He served on the faculties of Rutgers University and New York University, and he continued to be recognized for the impact *The Invisible Man* had on American society. He died at the age of 80 in Harlem.

Equiano, Olaudah (1745–97) was born in Essaka, an Igbo village in the kingdom of Benin (modern Nigeria). At the age of 11, he was kidnapped and sold into slavery. After 10 years of enslavement, he purchased his own freedom. He spent the next several years at sea and then returned to London where he met the British abolitionist, Granville Sharp. In 1789, he published his autobiography, which provided a model for the genre of the slave narrative. The work was one of the first to draw wide attention to the injustices of slavery.

Freud, Sigmund (1856–1939) was born in Freiberg, Moravia (now Pribor in the Czech Republic). His family moved to Vienna in 1860. He enrolled at the University of Vienna in 1873 and received his medical degree in 1881. In 1886, he established a private practice for the treatment of psychological disorders. His first book, *Studies in Hysteria*, written with his colleague Josef Breuer, was published in 1895. Shortly thereafter, Breuer found that he could not agree with Freud's emphasis on the sexual origin of neurosis, and the two parted. Freud continued to develop and publish his theories of psychoanalysis on his own. His major works include *The Interpretation of Dreams* (1900), *The Psychopathology of Everyday Life* (1901), and *Three Essays on the Theory of Sexuality* (1905). Although his work was not well received at first, he continued to write prolifically, and recognition of his work grew steadily until his death in 1939.

Gandhi, Mohandas K. (1869–1948) was born in 1869 to Hindu parents in the state of Gujarat in western India. His family later sent him to London to study law, and he received his degree 1891. He traveled to Southern Africa, where he spent more than two decades working to improve conditions for immigrant Indians. It was in Africa that he developed his method of passive resistance against injustice, *Satyagraha*, meaning truth force. He returned to India in 1915, where he took the lead in the long struggle for independence from Great Britain. Independence came in 1947. The last two months of his life were spent trying to end the violence between Hindu India and Muslim Pakistan. He fasted to the brink of death, an act that finally quelled the riots. In January 1948, at the age of 79, he was killed by an assassin as he walked through a crowded garden in New Delhi to take evening prayers. Gandhi has become revered as the father of Indian independence and one of the greatest spiritual and political leaders of modern times.

Heidegger, Martin (1889–1976) was born in Messkirch, Germany. He studied Roman Catholic theology and then philosophy at the University of Freiburg, where he was a student of Edmund Husserl, the founder of phenomenology. Heidegger became a professor of philosophy at Freiburg in 1928. His most significant work, *Being and Time* (1927), explored one of the essential questions of philosophy: What does it mean to be? He died in Messkirch on May 26, 1976.

Heisenberg, Werner (1901–76) was born in Würzburg, Germany. He showed a deep interest in physics throughout his schooling and studied with some of the most promising physicists of the day, most notably Niels Bohr. He invented matrix mechanics, the first formalization of quantum mechanics, in 1925. His Uncertainty Principle, discovered in 1927, states that determining the position and momentum of a particle necessarily contains errors, the product of which cannot be less than a known constant. Together with Bohr, he would go on to formulate the Copenhagen interpretation of quantum mechanics. He received the Nobel Prize in physics in 1932 "for the creation of quantum mechanics, the application of which has, *inter alia*, led to the discovery of the allotropic forms of hydrogen."

Hobbes, Thomas (1588–1679) was born in Wiltshire, England. At the age of 15, he began his studies at Oxford University. Throughout his life, Hobbes made many trips to mainland Europe where he met and corresponded with such thinkers as Galileo and René Descartes. Hobbes wrote on such subjects as the composition of matter and physics and especially human nature and political society. Hobbes's most well-known work, *Leviathan*, was one of two books condemned as blasphemous by the House of Commons in 1667.

King, Jr., Martin Luther (1929–68) was born in Atlanta, Georgia. His father and grandfather were Baptist ministers, and while attending Morehouse College, King made the decision to become a minister as well. In 1955, he received his doctorate in systematic theology from Boston College. It was while he was pastor at Dexter Avenue Baptist Church in Montgomery, Alabama, that King coordinated the boycott inspired by Rosa Parks's refusal to obey the city's mandated segregation on buses. In 1957, King and other civil rights activists founded the Southern Christian Leadership Conference. From 1957 to 1959, King wrote his first book, *Stride toward Freedom: The Montgomery Story*, and traveled to India, where he studied Gandhian nonviolent strategies. In 1963, King organized several large demonstrations, most famously those in Birmingham, Alabama, and Washington, D.C. King continued to lead hundreds of thousands of people in the civil rights movement until 1968, when he was assassinated in Memphis, Tennessee.

Malcolm X (1925–65) was born Malcolm Little on May 19, 1925, in Omaha, Nebraska. His mother, Louis Norton Little, was a homemaker occupied with the family's eight children. His father, Earl Little, was an outspoken Baptist minister and avid supporter of Black Nationalist leader Marcus Garvey. His father was murdered when Malcolm was six, and a turbulent childhood and adolescence followed. In 1946, he was convicted of burglary, and it was during his seven-year prison sentence that Malcolm further educated himself, became a follower of the Nation of Islam, and replaced his family name Little with the surname X. Always a controversial figure, his relationship with Elijah Muhammad (leader of the Nation of Islam) broke down after Malcolm X traveled to Mecca. He was assassinated in 1965.

Mencius (327–289 B.C.) was an ancient Chinese political theorist and follower of Confucianism. Mencius's political system of thought was based on *jen*—benevolence to one another. The degree of jen one displayed to a person was supposed to be in proportion to the relational obligations one held with the other. Like Confucius before him, Mencius was unsuccessful in influencing rulers with his political theory.

Mondrian, Piet (1872–1944) was born on March 7, 1872 in Amersfoort, Netherlands. He studied at the Amsterdam Academy from 1892 to 1895, then began painting on his own, focusing mainly on landscapes. In 1909, he began painting a series of trees, during the work on which he developed an increasingly abstract style. Around 1912, he moved to Paris where he was exposed to cubism. During World War I, Mondrian helped found *De Stijl*, a magazine of the arts that influenced European painting, architecture, and design. Mondrian called his style—characterized by thick black perpendicular lines and blocks of primary color—and its underlying artistic principles, "neoplasticism." His later paintings, which date from 1920 until his death, have simple titles, such as "Composition in Red, Yellow, and Blue," painted in 1926, and "Composition in White, Black, and Red" (1936).

Nicomachus (c. 60–120) was born in Roman Syria, now located in the modern city of Jarash, Jordan. A mathematician and Pythagorean, he believed that numbers had mystical significance. His book, *Introduction to Arithmetic*, was the first to treat arithmetic as a subject separate from geometry. Unlike Euclid, Nicomachus did not provide theoretical proofs of his theorems but simply stated them and provided numerical examples.

Nietzsche, Friedrich (1844–1900) was born in Prussia. He studied Greek and Latin at the University of Bonn and later at the University of Leipzig. In 1869, he was appointed professor of classical philology at the University of Basel in Switzerland. While at Basel, he became a close friend and admirer of the composer Richard Wagner and wrote *The Birth of Tragedy*, a work on the relationship of music and drama. Later, he had a falling out with Wagner on the importance of music. In 1879, he left Basel and began a decade of solitude during which he wrote *Beyond Good and Evil, Thus Spake Zarathustra*, and *The Will to Power*.

Pascal, Blaise (1623–62) was born in France in Clermont-Ferrand, Auvergne (now Clermont-Ferrand). He studied privately, tutored by his father. In 1631, the family moved to Paris and, in 1640, to Rouen. At the age of 16, he wrote his first significant mathematical treatise, *Essay pour les Coniques*, on conics. Together with Pierre de Fermat, Pascal invented the calculus of probabilities and laid foundations for Gottfried Wilhelm von Leibniz's infinitesimal calculus. In 1647, Pascal invented the calculating machine, and later the barometer, the hydraulic press, and the syringe. His most famous work, *Pensées*, is a collection of short writings compiled from his long search for theological truth.

Plato (427–347 B.C.) was born in Athens, where he spent his youth studying with the important teachers of Greece. He wrote tragedies until he met Socrates in 407. According to legend, he then burned all his poetry and turned to philosophy. After Socrates' death in 399, Plato began to write dialogues in which the character of Socrates plays the major role. In 388, he lived, taught, and studied at the court of Dionysius the Elder, ruler of Syracuse, Italy. When he returned to Athens, he founded the Academy, where a number of thinkers studied and taught mathematics and philosophy. His major works include *The Apology, The Meno, The Republic, The Sophist, The Timaeus*, and *The Phaedrus*. In 367 B.C., he returned to Sicily where he attempted to found a city that realized his ideas. When the experiment failed, he returned to Athens, where he lectured at the Academy until his death.

Poincaré, Henri (1854–1912) was born in Nancy, France. Educated in Paris, he became a professor of mathematics. He was one of the very few twentieth-century mathematicians who was also active in physics and astronomy as well as in almost all branches of mathematics. He was also unusual in his ability to write about highly technical matters in a way that was generally comprehensible.

Rousseau, Jean Jacques (1712–78) was born in Geneva, Switzerland. Rousseau left Geneva at age 16, spent the years of his 20s moving from place to place, and finally settled in Paris in 1742. He earned his living during this period by working as everything from a footman to an assistant to a French ambassador. In France, he met Voltaire and Diderot and contributed to the latter's *L'Encyclopedie*. A major figure of the Enlightenment, Rousseau first attracted wide attention with the *Discourse on the Sciences and the Arts* (1750). Other significant works include *Emile, or On Education* (1762), *Discourse on the Origin of Inequality* (1755), and *On the Social Contract* (1762).

Spinoza, Benedict (1632–77) was born in Amsterdam, Netherlands, into a Jewish family that had been exiled from Spain for religious reasons. He was raised with traditional Jewish schooling, but as an adult, Spinoza's budding theological speculations created conflict with Jewish leaders. He was banned from the synagogue in 1656 and left Amsterdam for a short period. In the two years after his return to Amsterdam, he wrote but did not publish *A Short Treatise on God, Man and His Well-Being, On the Improvement of the Understanding*, and his most significant work, *The Ethics*. In 1663, Spinoza left Rijnsburg and moved near The Hague. He hoped to publish *The Ethics*, but anticipating controversy, he instead wrote and anonymously published his *Tractatus Theologico-Politicus* (1670), which defends the liberty to philosophize in the face of religious or political interference.

Suzuki, Shunryu (1905–71) was a Japanese Zen priest belonging to the Soto lineage. He came to San Francisco in 1959, where he became the first abbot of Zen Center. Under his guidance, Zen Center expanded into City Center, Green Gulch Farm, and Tassajara Zen Mountain Center. He was one of the most influential Zen teachers of his time, and some of his edited talks have been collected in the books *Zen Mind, Beginner's Mind*, and *Branching Streams Flow in the Darkness: Zen Talks on the Sandokai*.

Theresa, Saint (1515–82) was a Carmelite nun and mystic who focused on reforming the order. She got her chance to do so in 1562 when she founded the convent of St. Joseph in Ávila. Her major works include *Life* (1565), *Way of Perfection* (c. 1565), *Interior Castle* (1577), and *The Foundations* (1582). Nearly 400 years after her death, Pope Paul VI declared Saint Theresa Ávila to be a doctor of the church—the first woman so ordained.

Thucydides (c. 460–400 B.C.) was born into a wealthy and influential family that owned homes in both Athens and Thrace. His family connections to both cities provided numerous occasions to connect with significant political figures. In 427, he contracted plague and recovered. Thucydides was in active service during the Peloponnesian War. He was made a general in 424 but failed to save Amphipolis from the Spartan general Brasidas, and Thucydides was exiled from Athens for seven years. As an Athenian exile, he was able to travel and to research war with the Peloponnesians. He returned to Athens in 404 and then to Thrace to work on his history of the war. The abrupt end of his work suggests that he may have died a sudden death, and there is strong evidence to suggest he did not live past 399.

Tung, Mao Tse (1893–1976) was born on December 26, 1893, in the home of a well-to-do peasant family in Hunan, China. In 1911, the imperial government was overthrown and, at seventeen, Mao became caught up in the political instability. After spending time in a revolutionary army, he began to study at a Hunan provincial library on his own and then joined a teaching course. In 1918, he went to Peking, where he befriended other radical Marxists and with them founded the Chinese Communist Party, the CCP. Mao proclaimed the People's Republic of China on October 1, 1949. He served as chairman of the CCP until 1959, when his initiative to force the peasantry into communes, called the "Great Leap Forward," proved to be disastrous. He was soon reinstated, however, and served as chairman of the CCP until his death in 1976.

Vermeer, Johannes (1632–75) was born in Delft, Netherlands, in 1632 and lived there until his death in 1675. No documents exist about his artistic training or apprenticeship, but it is likely that he trained in Delft, either with Leonaert Bramer (1596-1674) or Carel Fabritius (1622–54). Vermeer became a master in the Saint Luke's Guild on December 29, 1653. His first works were large-scale mythological and religious paintings. He then moved to the genre scenes, landscapes, and allegories for which he is best known.

Weil, Simone (1909–43) was born in Paris, France, in 1909. A member of a prosperous Jewish family, Weil studied at various schools before entering the Ecole Normale Supérieure in 1928. While at the university, Weil was exposed to many radical political beliefs and began developing her own views, which were largely influenced by Bolshevism. After graduating, she taught at various schools while working in a factory to examine the needs of the working class. In 1941, she lived briefly in the United States, but eagerly returned to London in November 1942 to take part in the French Resistance. She died of a combination of tuberculosis and anorexia in 1943. Writings published after her death included *Gravity and Grace* (1952) and *The Need for Roots* (1952).

Wilson, Woodrow (1856–1924) was born in Virginia. He studied at the College of New Jersey (now Princeton University) and entered the Law School at the University of Virginia in 1879. After a brief and unsuccessful law career, he entered Johns Hopkins University to prepare for a teaching career. He received his doctorate in 1886. He was a professor and then president at Princeton University until 1911, when he became governor of New Jersey. In 1912, he was elected the 28th president of the United States and served until 1920. He initiated the formation of the League of Nations after World War I and is credited with defining the modern era of U.S. foreign policy.

Wittgenstein, Ludwig (1889–1951) was born in Vienna, Austria. Wittgenstein studied mechanical engineering in Berlin. In 1908, he went to Manchester, England, to do research in aeronautics—in particular, experimenting with kites. He met the mathematician and philosopher Gottlob Frege (1848–1925), who recommended that he study with Bertrand Russell (1872–1970) in Cambridge. At Cambridge University, Wittgenstein focused on logic and, with Russell's help, he published *Tractatus Logico-Philosophicus* in 1922. By 1949, he had written all the material included in *Philosophical Investigations*, arguably his most important work. His collected work from the last two years of his life has been published as *On Certainty*.

Wollstonecraft, Mary (1759–97) was born in London, England. Her family moved often while she was growing up. She left home in 1778 to become a lady's companion. In 1784, Wollstonecraft became involved with a group known as the "Rational Dissenters," led by Richard Price. This involvement exposed her to many leading radicals of the day, including Josef Johnson. Johnson was impressed by Wollstonecraft's ideas on education and commissioned her first book, *Thoughts on the Education of Daughters* (1786). *The Female Reader* was published in 1789, and *A Vindication of the Rights of Women* was published in 1792. In 1797, Wollstonecraft became pregnant and married William Godwin. She gave birth to Mary Godwin Shelly in August. Wollstonecraft died from complications of childbirth.

Woolf, Virginia (1882–1941) was born and raised in London, England. She led a turbulent life, during which she had multiple psychological breakdowns. Recognized in her own time and since her death as one of the most significant novelists of the modern era, her stream-of-consciousness style captured the political, philosophical, historical, and materialist issues of her time. Her most famous works include Mrs. Dalloway (1925), To the Lighthouse (1927), Orlando: A Biography (1928), The Waves (1931), and her most-recognized work, A Room of One's Own (1929).